be free

hiking the colorado trail

starroute.net

Meachele *mothership* Montgomery

be free
hiking the colorado trail

by Meachele Mothership Montgomery

Copyright © 2016 – Meachele Mothership Montgomery

ISBN: 978-1-5309-7775-8

First printing, April 2016

www.starroutebooks.net

starroute.net

an imprint of Imaging Specialists, Inc.

"Living in
two worlds is
exhausting.
And impossible
long term.
Take time to
mentally
get yourself
off the trail.
But also,
try things.
Try to find what
the next thing is.
Not to escape,
but the next
means for
discovery."

Sarah *patchouli* Binger
AT NOBO 2013

To all the victims who need to be free.

Meachele *mothership* Montgomery

foreword

Life has an interesting way of showing each of us direction and purpose even during what we may feel is our darkest and most hopeless days. Few people ever achieve a life free of pain, trauma or tragedy. Others are blessed to only experience faith, hope and love. Meachele "Mothership" Montgomery has proven to be a blessing in disguise for many people as she has experienced the best-of-the-best and the-worst-of-the-worst in her lifetime. She has emerged through all of the trials and tribulations life has thrust upon her and she continues to bloom as a survivor, writer, mother, dedicated hiker, friend and a beautiful inspiration and example of how to come through the darkest of days and find a reason to continue on.

I have never physically met Meachele face-to-face or even spoken to her on the phone. Our friendship, and ensuing email exchanges, bloomed out of a shared experience and pain due to the death of our spouses. An article about "healing...My Journey Home", was published in the local/community paper back in April 2015, just as I was coming up on the one-year mark of being a young widow. Just as you are reading this foreword, you can understand and appreciate the magical way Meachele shared her journey through the Appalachian Trail and found her way home to continue on in her life.

Fast forward to February 2016...I received an email from Meachele asking if I would have time to read a draft of her second book. Meachele asked me to think about the following four issues as I read the draft. She wanted this second book to achieve a few key points as she moved through the next chapter of her journey:

- Is the book worth reading?
- Will someone get something out of it?
- Will it hurt others?
- Is God glorified in this book?

As you read Meachele's second book, I encourage you to keep these four questions in the forefront of your mind. I promise you will find several passages, which speak directly to you and the initial reason you read her first book and joined in her journey through the Appalachian Trail.

That being said, there are several passages in Meachele's second story which have caused me to pause and really think about my own life and where I am in my journey, however the one below has become my compass as I continue forward in my journey:

"Life's valleys can be cold as well, but with prayer and help we can overcome many obstacles. An individual must desire to change and practice change. As youngsters we're told, "Practice makes perfect." And that continues throughout our lives. Are you a willing vessel?"

Meachele, thank you for having the courage to share your journey. You have given me hope, direction and a reason and purpose to continue to move forward with my own journey. Life can be many things to many people, however my life is enriched and beautifully blessed because you have shared so much of your soul.

Tammy L. Thiele
Valle Crucis, NC
April 18, 2016

rerun

"Set up camp now!" I heard a voice say.

"Okay, but you know how I dislike doing that in the rain," I replied.

I was at almost 13,000 feet, and it had been raining for two days. I had reached the last climb in the section going to Stony Pass Trailhead on the Colorado Trail, and I was certain that I could hike the last bit to the jeep trail, where I could possibly find someone to hitch a ride with. But that voice inside me said, "Now!"

I quickly checked out my surroundings to find a place to set up my two-man tent. There wasn't a lot of acceptable ground to choose from. Sheep poop and rocky surfaces dominated the area. It was a difficult task and needed immediate attention.

Settling for an area about ten feet from the pond, five feet from the six-foot-tall rock formation, and free of sheep feces, I rapidly went to my black backpack covered with my black waterproof pack cover that I had dropped a few minutes earlier. The clouds continued to expel liquid on me. There was no letting up that day.

After retrieving the footprint for the tent, rainfly, stakes, and poles, I worked swiftly because my extremities were becoming numb from being wet and cold for the last few hours. I laid the footprint down and snapped the pole sections into place, and then was ready to place the three ends into the footprint. The frame was up, and I draped the rainfly on the frame. I staked the rainfly down, then unzipped the door and placed my backpack inside the tent. I slid in behind the pack, ready to take a short breather. I was finally out of the rain.

Pulling the inside of the tent from my pack, I was able to clip the six hooks to the frame. I needed to secure the four ends, so I slipped under the rainfly. After attaching the ends to the stakes already in place, I was almost ready to call it a day. The tent was anchored for the night.

My next task was to remove my wet clothes and find dry clothes in my orange stuff sac. I had hiked almost 12 miles that day and just over 17 miles the day before in the freezing rain, and both pairs of socks were wet. My feet were waterlogged and needed to warm up. Pulling out my green and black snoveler (a 20-degree down quilt cover that can be worn as a poncho because it has a slit in the middle), I wrapped my feet up. After heating up two cups of water, I placed a package of dehydrated food between my legs and waited until it was ready to eat. It had two purposes that day - to warm me externally and internally. I opened my survival blanket pack and wrapped myself in it before covering my body with my quilt. I was wearing a merino wool top, Sherpa fleece pants, and a red down jacket. Finally dry, I wanted to take a nap.

But, no, a lightning storm of massive caliber surrounded me! Through my tent, I could see the heavens illuminated with every color of the rainbow, and the chariots of thunder racing across the sky were deafening. Never have I seen or heard a storm that intense! I laid flat and covered my eyes with my hands.

I had just heard that a hiker was killed by lightning a few mountains over. And another couple were hit and survived, but their dog died. The guidebook for the Colorado Trail recommends that hikers start early in the day and descend by early afternoon if on exposed ridges. Storms tend to brew around 2 p.m., but I was in several that started in the morning and late afternoon. I learned to watch the cloud patterns all day long.

I had been above 12,000 feet all morning, and the rain was coming down so heavily that I didn't think a lightning storm would follow. The sky can change so rapidly that an escape route is difficult to find. Life can seem like that at times, but often there is a way to safety. I had listened to the inner voice that said, "Set up camp now!"

It continued to rain throughout the night, and I frequently checked to see if the pond water was inching toward the tent. I prayed that there was a run-off, and that it wasn't in my direction!

It was a cold and wet night. Perfect conditions for hypothermia. Would my sons hear about a hiker perishing during a monsoon? Monsoons are supposed to happen only in the South Pacific!

Locals had said, "The season of extreme rain has started early this year." Heavy rains usually start in August. This was August 2, and I'd been in a few milder storms up to that point.

On my thru-hike (hiking a complete trail in one season) of the Appalachian Trail in 2011, I encountered hazardous conditions on several occasions. One such time was during my shakedown (a hike on which you test your gear to make sure everything is working properly). I was hiking during a blizzard and conditions became dangerous very quickly. The snow was falling rapidly and the temperature dropped speedily. Hiking off the mountaintop in the fading light was risky. But I knew this area of Mount Rogers, Virginia. This was where I had hiked several times a week to attain some form of fitness before hitting the Appalachian Trail in early March 2011. During this blizzard event, I prayed that my sons wouldn't find me frozen to a tree as I navigated my way down the five-mile trail to my car. With me, I had my trusted hiking companion, Cianna, my then almost two-year-old Spinone, who guided me safely down the mountain. Following her moving white body, I reached the car just after 9 p.m.

But I was on my own on this occasion. Cianna wouldn't have survived all the lightning storms that came with this adventure on the Colorado Trail.

As I drifted in and out of sleep, I prayed that the Forest Rangers or other hikers wouldn't find me frozen in my tent. I had taken every precaution to ensure my safety that afternoon, from setting up camp and putting on dry clothes to eating a hot meal. The rest was out of my control.

why this book?

I thought I knew what this next book was going to be about. But little did I know that my life would change again on July 17, 2015. That was the day when God started showing me that it was time to share my hurts, abuses, and other events that have shaped who I am today. After keeping things to myself for so many years, I didn't know how I would share things that people were unwilling to hear.

Since I believe that the church is the hospital, I could never understand why it was so difficult for church people to speak of abuse. The thief on the cross asked to be remembered, but who thinks of the victims? We say we're "fine" when someone asks. We're reluctant to state our true feelings because we wonder if anyone really wants to hear what we have to say. Do you have the time or the desire to genuinely concentrate on me and what I have to say?

I attended a meeting the other night, and the people were interested in each other's affairs. Some people spoke and others listened; individuals took turns sharing their concerns and fears. It was breathtaking to hear the deep thoughts and life lessons that came from these people. One person said, "The word, 'should', has a hold on me. I hear that I 'should' do this or I 'shouldn't' do that." She went on and stated that living in the here and now is what helps her.

That's all well and good, but many individuals have been hurt as youngsters and they're unable to process that effectively. The bottled-up experiences have become a deep-rooted cancer. They re-live and think about those events continuously. My oldest son and my mom said a similar thing just days apart, "Don't dwell on the past. Just move forward." That's easier said than done. Have they experienced the things others have? People are quick to say something and they have no idea what a person has gone through. I want to be a listener, keep my mouth shut, and refrain from giving my two cents.

Studies show that a childhood trauma can affect the mental growth of an individual if the events aren't dealt with. If something tragic takes place at the age of 11, that child could have a difficult time processing the future. That's understandable because what we learn first is hard to erase and relearn.

Why this book? As I continued hiking, the Lord kept telling me that victims need to find "freedom." They need individuals who will hear them out and encourage them that they can make it through the hard times. They need to know that there are others out there who have been through similar incidents. They are not alone.

We're hesitant to listen when someone starts communicating uncomfortable topics. Our radar goes up and it's easier to walk away. Who wants to hear about sexual or physical abuse or that a dad could have been a pedophile? Psychologists and the system want families to stay together and work through issues. But how can anyone work through these things when our children are raised in a protective environment? They should be able to run free and be raised by everyone in the neighborhood. But no, we keep them so close and rarely let them explore the world.

be free

I grew up running around the village in Germany. Every-one knew me as "the American." For the most part, I was safe. My friends and I would play in the fields and barns and spend hours at the swimming pool. We migrated home for lunch and met up again in the afternoon. That is how I spent many summers in my beloved village, Langensteinbach.

There are some individuals who are capable of evil and do unthinkable things. As a Christian, I believe that people can change. I have a hope that individuals want to be good. The Lord knows their hearts, and they will be judged.

the snake

As a long distance hiker, my feet start itching in early spring to hit a trail somewhere. I had helped a friend who goes by the trail name of Corona Sam as he was attempting a thru-hike on the Appalachian Trail in 2012. In 2015, he asked if I would like to hike the Colorado Trail. My ears perked up at that possibility. Interest in hiking out west grew quickly and I ordered guidebooks.

Facebook and e-mail messages were exchanged concerning plans and possible dates. My husband, Tom, whom I had married the past October, was on board. So we hit the gym several times a week to train for this adventure.

The Colorado Trail would be a 484-mile trek that would take us from Denver to Durango, Colorado, reaching 13,271 feet at its highest elevation. Low altitude is defined as below 7,000 feet. I live near 3,000 feet. So the altitude was going to be an issue.

Being newlyweds, we needed the time together and this seemed like the perfect thing. Since Tom enjoyed his motorcycle, we decided to ride to Utah before starting our summer adventure on the trail.

On the last weekend in June, we attended church before hitting the open road headed west. It was a warm, sunny day, and we allocated a week for travel time. We had mailed three resupplies (food and other supplies you need on the trail during your hike) to Corona Sam's cabin. Our other items were packed on the bike.

There isn't an easy way out of the mountains of Western North Carolina. Our GPS took us over "The Snake" in Tennessee. It's a road that many bikers enjoy riding - 33 miles long with 489 curves that travels over three mountains and through one valley. I'm a new rider, and I'm not too crazy about speed. So, it was a huge decision on my part to travel on the back of my husband's bike. I wanted to develop trust.

It's wonderful to experience the wind blowing in your face, feeling like you are part of everything around you. But it's also a scary feeling not being in control. You're helpless as the driver has your life in his hands. You're passing eighteen-wheelers at 70 and 80 miles an hour, and there's nothing between you and them. I never kept my eyes closed as tightly as I did then! I sat ever so still and prayed. This form of traveling wasn't my first choice, but I wanted to please my husband.

When the road was free of other drivers, I enjoyed being on the bike. I had been riding horses for years and experienced the same freedom as I galloped them across the fields or on the beaches of Cornwall, England. I never liked being around other riders either. Having some distance between you and other people can be a good thing.

Individual space is something I taught my kindergartners at the Arts and Basic Charter School in Wilkesboro, North Carolina. Arms extended - that's my space and you don't need to be in it. If we followed that thought process, there might be fewer issues and accidents.

As my son said, "Mom, there's just no need to drive so fast. You're not going to get there any sooner." What will it take for people to slow down?

relationships

After graduating from the University of Chapel Hill in North Carolina, I was commissioned in the United States Navy. My first duty station was Brawdy, Wales. It was time for me to become an adult and find my way in this world.

Setting out in the spring of 1982, I would be in charge of my future and live with the consequences of my decisions. I met my first husband, Ray, at this naval facility that was out in the middle of nowhere. The area hasn't changed in thirty years. If you've ever watched *All Creatures Great and Small*, that's how the area of Southwest Wales still looks. It's a wonderful place to raise children and enjoy the simple things in life, family, and friends.

Ray and I were married there in a small Welsh chapel and after our third son was born, we had the pleasure of returning there for another assignment. Our three-year orders turned into five years. The boys learned how to ride horses and competed in horse shows and pony rallies.

Our twenty-seven years together came to an early end when my husband was diagnosed with kidney cancer. His kidney was removed, but the disease had spread. We had a year after his operation. Special memories were added to the many other ones that we had created over the years. In all the years we were together, we never fought.

In January 2014, I met Tom. He had served in the Armed Forces, liked the outdoors, and was willing to relocate. All this sounded promising, and we started dating in spite of the five-hour driving distance. In no time, I was falling for this kind person, and the week before Easter, he asked me to marry him. My granddaughters loved him and that was enough for me.

After a 2014 hiking trip on the Camino de Santiago, Spain, we came back to North Carolina and started thinking of our future together. He sold his house in Kentucky and moved to North Carolina. We started riding horses together and planned to build a small cabin near the New River where we bought a piece of property.

Our wedding date was set for October 10, 2014, and we were excited about spending our future together in the mountains of North Carolina. It was a colorful fall and although the day was scattered with showers, it was a wonderful wedding with family and friends. The small chapel had been built on top of a mountain by the developer of the Deerwood Park Community and the Barn was the perfect place to host our reception.

Appalachian Trail hiking pals drove from Michigan and Washington, D.C., to be a part of the event. We had made the floral arrangements from flowers we had picked and dried. The whole family was involved in the wedding preparations - truly a family affair.

The special day arrived and my friend, Sandy, whom I met on the Appalachian Trail in 2011, came to be my maid of honor. She was my trail angel (a person who does kind things for hikers) on the AT and she was there to support me in my new adventure.

I wanted the wedding party and friends to walk to the chapel. It's a tradition from my German heritage, and I envisioned doing that on my wedding day. It didn't happen, but Sandy and I walked to the chapel together. She gave me a blue umbrella to carry through the spitting rain, and we had the best time singing as we proceeded to the chapel.

As we neared the steps, my two older granddaughters came down to escort me to the chapel door. My two older sons, Bradley and Shaun, were singing on the porch, and my granddaughter, Harley, helped me up the steps. We then separated as the aisle on the side was too small for two people. She walked to the front, and as my sons completed the song, I walked up. Bradley's wife, Jessica, and Tom's daughter lit the family candles while Eric, my youngest son, helped with the communion. Kayleigh, my youngest granddaughter, carried the heart-shaped ring holder. It was a fairy tale wedding that ended with a meal and dancing. More relationships were being formed as the two extended families joined that day.

We had a rough time in spite of the beautiful beginning. Tom had moved to North Carolina where he knew no one and had given up his way of life in Kentucky to live close to my family members. My sons each have a cabin that they built with their father on this three-acre lot. We see each other often and there is no getting away from that. It's something he wasn't accustomed to. His brother had lived next to their parents for years, but Tom lived nearly two hours away. You learn to accept such an arrangement or it becomes an issue very quickly.

It developed into an issue because Tom would say, "Everyone is using you." If I don't feel used and I'm willing to do it, then why should it matter? After we were married, other concerns started surfacing. It seemed as though he would start something every week that would end up in an argument with no solutions. Not familiar with such behavior, I tried to have reasonable discussions, but that didn't work, so

I would become withdrawn. I would shut down and refuse to quarrel. I can dispense with "drama."

I prayed and gave it much thought before asking him to leave in February 2015. We were apart for five weeks, and he continued to call and send text messages. I agreed to meet on one of his trips to North Carolina, willing to give us a second chance. There were several things I had to forgive him for: taking money out of the bank account before I said anything about him leaving, the way he said, "You only get a kiss when you deserve it," and how he made me feel cheap when I was cleaning or picking up something from the floor by saying, "If you're down there, why not give me a blow job?" I understand that men need sex, but they don't need to make everything about sex. There are other things in this world to talk about and do besides sex.

We agreed to start a marriage class at church, and we read our homework together. The six-week course was informative, but true change comes only with practice. It has to become part of your daily life. I'm not perfect, but I try to be the best I can be. Being told when you're trying, "You're so perfect," in a sarcastic voice or belittling tone, is degrading.

The old saying is, "Sticks and stones may break your bones, but names will never hurt you." In reality, verbal abuse can haunt you for a lifetime. I can remember my first mother-in-law saying, "When you move back to the United States, the boys won't need a grandma." I was heartbroken that she thought that. And my second mother-in-law asked me, "What did you do?" Why is it my fault that someone else lost control? Words hurt, and they can play havoc in our minds.

Before traveling west, my mom said, "Love him." That had always been my goal, but I needed to work through my feelings and thoughts. Would he act that way again? Were the arguments going to start for no reason? Would he listen to anything I said? Nervousness set in. I would continue to work on this relationship because I believe in love and marriage.

However, other relationships come and go. Medicineman, whom I met before my Appalachian Trail hike said, "Some people come into your life and then they leave." I found this unnerving for a long time, but as I continued my hike north on the AT, I began to understand and accept this phrase, and it's part of my life now. There are people I will meet and have only a short connection with, and that's okay. We aren't required to remain chums forever. People with different interests, likes, and dislikes make a creative and beautiful world for us to live in.

Corona Sam fell into the category of short acquaintance. Yes, I helped him in 2012, and he graciously invited us to hike the Colorado Trail and took care of all the resupplies.

But because Tom and I weren't keeping up with his itinerary, he left a message for me on a post. It stated, "Doesn't seem like you can hike close to any speed to get the miles I set out to match my food days. This is all screwed up now. I'm not certain what to say. Basically trip is ruined for us all if you are not in hiker shape." He continued in a second note, "I guess we should have talked more about our hiking styles. I had told everyone that I get up early due to storms. I hike only about 1.9 - 2 mph with breaks." Even though we had three extra days, his agenda allowed no room for adjustment.

I'm 56 years old, and I'm not willing to spend a vast amount of time waiting for possible changes in people's behavior. There is too much to see and experience. Time is running out and I want to be around people who are positive, self-motivated, and happy. I can't fix anyone.

A friend, whom I know only through Facebook, John Forbes, says it so well, "My inner circle has been trimmed, and I am finding that I no longer waste my time on what I will refer to as the wrong people. For some a lifetime is spent in cliques that serve to tear down and distract. The best thing that any of us can ever do in life is surround ourselves exclusively with folks of similar bents that lift us up rather than push us off."

Recently, I learned about "Earth People." These individuals are born with a natural high and are called "happy" people. I always wondered why I was so easily pleased with the simple things in life. Now I know. My granddaughter said years ago, "Nana Meachele, you're just too HAPPY!" What a great compliment!

gear

When I first started hiking and backpacking, I read books and quickly realized there was much more to this hobby then just walking in the woods. On day hikes, you can carry as little or as much as you like, knowing that you are homeward bound at the end of the day. But when staying in the wilderness for days on end, you need much more. So I picked the brains of those who had been doing it for years.

Grits and Medicineman were two individuals whom I met on whiteblaze.net, a web site for Appalachian Trail hiking enthusiasts. Mike, who was then employed by our local outfitting store, became my go-to guy for questions and/or concerns about backpacking.

On my first shakedown hike on Mt. Rogers, I nearly burned the forest down with my cooking setup. It was the kind that you need to pump and regulate the fuel flow - something that was too difficult for me. Instead, I nearly melted the fuel bottle! I moved quickly to place the fuel bottle and stove into a fire pit where it finally ran out of fuel. Upon returning to town, I went to Mike.

"Mike, I need something simple for cooking," I said.

Mike helped with my next method of cooking and Medicineman was all about lightening my load. My gear has evolved over time. The older and heavier packs were sold to boy scouts who were just starting off on their camping adventures as I learned to select lighter gear.

For my Appalachian Trail journey, I used a Warbonnet Double-layer Blackbird hammock at 40 ounces with an Outdoor Equipment Supplier MacCat Deluxe 130"x104" tarp at 12.5 ounces and a ULA Circuit backpack at 41 ounces. When using a hammock, I have a Jacks 'R' Better 25-30 degree Snoveller at 24 ounces, which is my top quilt, and a Hammock Gear ¾ Phoenix 20-degree under-quilt at 17.6 ounces which hangs under my hammock to stop the air flow. With all of these items, I carry around 8 ½ pounds.

If your five main items, which include your shelter, backpack, sleeping bag, pad if using a tent, and cooking setup, together weigh around ten pounds, you are on your way to getting your pack lighter. On the Colorado Trail, I was using a Big Agnes Ultralight Fly Creek 2-person tent at 2 pounds 5 ounces and a Q-Core Superlight pad with an estimated R-Value of 4.5 at 1 pound.

You're not going to save weight going to a hammock over tenting. But I find that I sleep much better in a hammock and things stay cleaner. My dog can sleep under the hammock and not in my sleeping bag in the tent. However, it was nice being in a shelter during the rain storms on the Colorado Trail. There are pros and cons to either method of backpacking you choose. The terrain dictates which mode will best suit your venture.

In life as in backpacking, we try to choose what is best for us. It's your life and your adventure. Do your own hike. Find what works for you and change the things you can change.

prep/skill

When I was in the hospital in Bermuda giving birth to my third son, I had a roommate who was only 15 years old at the time. She shared how it was customary for islanders to have a child at a young age. Her grandmother, mother, sisters, and other family members were all young when they had their first child. It was difficult for me to understand this practice since I was 31 years old when my last son was born.

It struck me as odd then and I'm still shocked that it's easier to have a child then it is to adopt a dog in this country. Training in parenthood has fallen by the wayside. With the negation of the extended family in the 1950s, we have missed out on having grandparents, aunties, uncles, and older cousins around to help raise our children. The sharing of knowledge and skills among family members has become a lost art. We seek the help of others to become mentors to those who have no one in their lives. Even with all the self-help books, there are people who aren't receiving the training or skills needed to become positive and self-reliant individuals.

Skills and preparation time are required to excel at most things. As I became interested in long distance hiking, I longed for understanding and experience. Finding information wasn't the issue because there is so much available on this topic. Narrowing it down to what worked for me was more challenging. Through trial and error, I found the right backpack and learned to listen to my body.

During my fitness training for the Appalachian Trail, I read something in Eric Jardin's book about walking 500 miles before starting any long hike. It made perfect sense to walk in order to be fit and ready for a 2,000-mile hike. I started walking after my husband died in September 2010, and I was ready for the mountains in GA. Others I knew hiked fewer miles and experienced injuries early on. After all of the walking and training, I felt that the physical side would be doable. The mental aspect of that monumental task was something else.

How does one prepare mentally for a long distance hike? Hiking alone only adds to that issue. On my first long distance hike, I had my companion Cianna, and she proved to be a vital part in keeping me focused on the mission at hand. Having her to talk to, I was able to make the miles and days go by.

The knowledge that she would protect me in the woods was added comfort. We, as humans, want to be loved and protected. Cianna provided both. Man's best friend is a dog! For 1,200 miles on the Appalachian Trail, she was, and still is, my best friend. That unconditional love is shown to me daily. But how do you overcome the mental difficulties of the trail or life in general? It's a battle that everyone faces at some point in their life.

With the busyness of life, family and friends aren't always available to listen or help with one's situations. So it's important that we learn to love our own company. Can you be alone and accomplish assignments? A self-motivated individual is a great asset to an employer. Liking yourself and your own company can make dealing with the mental stress of long distance hiking easier.

An individual whom I met on the Colorado Trail messaged me on Facebook the other day. It said, "I just emailed Chris and he made it to Buena Vista, but everyone else bailed except you, I think. He quit because there was no one else out there and he was too lonely. Said he'd pass a NOBO (a north bounder or someone hiking a trail north) every couple days but no conversation for two and a half weeks got to him."

That hiker wasn't able to deal with the loneliness that can come with long distance hiking. He completed 216 of the 484 miles. The Appalachian Trail sees a drop-out rate of 25% in the first 30 miles and another 25% before the half-way point. And a lot of that is to do with not being able to handle hiking unaccompanied for long periods of time.

I have found that a positive, happy, go-with-the-flow type of individual seems to have a better chance at completing a long distance hike. It could be that we worry less and experience less fear of things that could or do go wrong. We are in the moment and enjoy what life brings us. Mentally, I'm able to cope with much, but physically, I need to prepare for each hike.

Just as I continue to learn about new gear, I gain skills as a hiker that prove to be helpful on other hikes and in life in general. Wisdom learned from and freely given by the trail is something for each of us to embrace. Being your own and only companion for three or more weeks can be rewarding or destructive. You also have a choice in life. You can become a valuable, positive, and self-motivated person or someone who others refuse to be around because you are so negative and suck the life out of people.

Having all the right gear doesn't mean that you will complete an entire trail; however, you can learn and continue to follow your dream. It may be that you're able to hike only short sections of trails and that's your goal. The key is to prepare and gain the skills needed to achieve your aspirations.

three days

It was essential for me to have a high level of fitness this past summer since I was hiking with three male hikers. Two had thru-hiked the Appalachian Trail and the other was a day hiker. As we set off on July 4, 2015, the trail proved to be a challenge right from the start. Hiking just over 10 miles on the first day, we encountered heat and the need to carry water. The dirt road that followed the river for a long while radiated heat up through the soles of our shoes. Several hikers developed blisters within miles of stepping on the Colorado Trail.

Upon seeing our first Bighorn Sheep, we stopped and took several pictures. I had already halted to capture some wildflowers blooming on the side of the trail on my new Samsung camera. We decided to stop and replenish our water supply after hiking through the heat and taking several breaks. The Colorado Trail Databook, a small pack guide that divides the trail into sections, states, "Be aware that the next reliable water source is more than 8 miles away."

It was essential for Tom to doctor up his blistered feet and have a rest. Before continuing on, I cooked dinner and treated our water. We sat on a log and several other hikers that we had met during the day decided to eat dinner as well. Our initial dinner conversation was, "Where are you from? Why are you hiking the trail? How heavy is your pack?"

As we were finishing our first cooked meal on the trail, the rain set in and we proceeded to climb the last few miles through thick brush. We were disappointed that we had carried a large amount of water up the final incline of the day since there was ample water after the 8.7-mile mark. With each liter weighing over two pounds, a backpack quickly becomes heavier with each added liter of water. I had over two liters and Tom packed out over three liters.

Daylight was fading, and we were ready to stop after hiking just over 10 miles on the first day. We came around the last bend to see two tents and two familiar faces - Grizzle and Corona Sam. I set up our tent just below theirs and it wasn't long until I said goodnight and went to sleep. There was no shortage of water at this campsite. We could fill up in the morning.

The next day we would be hiking at over 7,000 feet and after leaving the South Platte River Trailhead, we could be without a reliable water source for 13 miles. Grizzle and Corona Sam were out of camp early. They liked rising at 4:30 a.m. and hitting the trail shortly thereafter. I have always been happy to leave camp around 6:30 a.m. and hike all day long, stopping whenever I like.

Up and ready to hike on a cooler morning, we set foot on the trail at 6 a.m. After climbing for 3 miles, we were ready for the 4.2-mile decent to the Gudy Gaskill Bridge. As Tom soaked his feet in the river, I treated our water and prepared our lunch. While we sat eating in the shade, we saw several tourists with kayaks, bikers who were cycling the Colorado

Trail, and day hikers. We saw thru-hikers often in the first few days of starting the trail and then the bubble began. Groups of people move forward on the trail and you may never see the other hikers because you're hiking the same miles each day. This particular afternoon, we saw two middle-aged women who were section hiking (hiking only a part of a trail) and we never saw them again.

After our break, we started another steady 6-mile climb that reached almost 8,000 feet. With our bodies fueled up and our backpacks heavy with added water, we started the climb. It was slightly overcast which helped as we crossed the "burnt section." A fire in 1996 burned some 12,000 acres making this a difficult stretch because it lacks shade and water.

Many wildflowers have flourished since the fire. I took every opportunity to snap photos - the blue columbine which is Colorado's state flower, paintbrush, buckwheat, and sunflowers. As I viewed the beauty around, I took some items from Tom's pack and hoped this would make the hike easier

on him. I carried the tent and the food in order to get his pack weight to 18 pounds without water. He started with 3 liters most days. Starting in the morning, his pack would weigh just under 25 pounds.

As we continued in the burnt area, we never really knew how far we had come. We finally reached an opening where I could see a road sign. My journal entry for that evening stated, "Oh, no! We're only at the 6-mile mark." We had hiked just over 6 miles in each of sections 1 and 2 from the Colorado Trail Databook, for a total of 12.8 miles that day. Tom was done, and it had rained for the last two miles. We stopped at Raleigh Peak Road, and I set up the tent in the mist.

Hoping I had enough water left for the 4 miles to the firehouse because Tom had drunk his 3 liters, I checked my supply. Luckily, I had packed out 2 ¼ liters, and I had 17 ounces left. It was just after 7 p.m. and Tom was already asleep. Eating no dinner, I also fell asleep shortly thereafter.

July 6th began with a misty morning. As Tom was tending to his feet, I packed up the tent and decided to hike in my wool sleeping top because my hiking shirt was still wet. On the Appalachian Trail, I often put on my wet clothes to start the day off hiking. I just can't bring myself to do that anymore!

Leaving the quietness of the dirt road, we continued hiking through the burnt area with only 17 ounces of water between us. We had not reached the 19-mile goal yesterday. Would the others wait on us? Tom's feet needed a few days off the trail. I tried to cheer him up but it became a very difficult task. As I shared my last sip of water, I knew I was taking care of two hikers.

We came around a large rock formation, and I saw a house in the distance. Overjoyed, I told Tom.

Tom's response was, "That's another mile away."

I decided to hike ahead. After finding an emergency water supply, I filled up my bottle, dropped my backpack, and headed back to Tom. I handed him the water bottle and took his pack. We walked together and reached the 6 gallons of water that were in a plastic crate.

The sign stated in large red lettering, "Emergency water." And the second line in blue lettering stated, "Please conserve."

After a hot lunch, we needed to discuss our next step in this adventure.

I asked, "What do you want to do?"

The first thing out of his mouth was, "I'm going home."

"Why?" I questioned.

Nothing. I continued to ask.

He finally said, "Walk."

Tom handed me the stove. So now I was carrying the tent, stove, and all the food.

I packed up my gear and started walking very slowly to the trailhead that was 1.4 miles away. I saw a note in a sandwich bag secured to the rusty pole with duct tape, so I dropped my pack and sat against a tree to read it. It was from Corona Sam. As I waited for Tom, I read it several times. After waiting for an hour, I finally asked two hikers if they had passed anyone.

"No, we haven't passed anyone all day," they responded.

Had Tom decided to hitch a ride to the first food drop and rest his feet there? Or was he heading home? I could only assume that he was heading for the food drop at Kenosha Pass some 45 miles away. After reading Corona Sam's note again, I became obsessed with the goal to reach his camp that night.

Could I hike 18 more miles before nightfall? I was seeing red as I rehearsed my speech. How could he think I misled him on being able to hike this trail? Or question if I was in hiker shape? How dare he offend me in this manner!

I notched off the miles. I don't recall what I saw on that afternoon hike. While resting at Redskin Trail, I asked a biker what time it was.

"It's 3:34 p.m.," he stated.

I could do another 7.5 miles before dark. After hiking 22.2 miles on the 3rd day, I arrived and stood in front of Corona Sam's tent after greeting Grizzle. I was ready to unload everything that had been on my mind for the last 7 hours.

"You made it," he said.

"I'm offended that you would think I have misled you about being able to hike the Colorado Trail," I started, "I hiked over 22 miles! I think I'm in hiker shape."

I continued, "You knew Tom had blisters and how difficult it is for him to hike. But no, it's your way or the highway. Yet you want someone around in case you blow your knee."

He let out a chuckle, saying, "We have blisters, and we could have done more miles."

I then told him that I just wanted the map or for him to write down where the food drops were located. Then he and Grizzle wouldn't have to worry about us any longer.

Finally, I declared that he should never invite anyone else to hike with him. I had gotten everything off my chest, and I was at peace with what I said. We can allow people to affect our state of mind if they have offended us in some way. And it's important to try and resolve issues, but some people just haven't the skills or desire to settle matters because they may think there is no problem or it's all your problem. Maybe you just don't have the time to work things out. This is why I move people to the "I know you but we're not going to have a close relationship" category. And that's okay because I would rather have one true unconditional friendship than a million acquaintances.

I experience those unconditional connections with my three adult sons. No matter what happens in life, they are there for me and I am there for them. They are the reason I continue to press on in this world because I want to be an example for them. That inner peace that comes from God, I can show and share with others. I'm happy just because, but I'm also better at sharing my hurts and concerns with others.

continental divide

Our words are so powerful. The Bible says, "And the tongue is a fire, a world of iniquity." The word "iniquity" is defined as immoral or grossly unfair behavior. The Bible teaches that nothing can cause more damage than the tongue, and that we need to learn how to keep our speech under control. This can be difficult, but criticism, slander, backbiting, and gossip can destroy relationships. That doesn't mean we stop trying to communicate our hurts, concerns, and desires in a more positive way.

Have you ever met someone who doesn't want to listen to your point of view? Just think about your so-called friends or members in your own family who are uncomfortable to be around because they refuse to listen to you or acknowledge your perspective. You weren't heard as a youngster and now that you're an adult, they still reject your thoughts.

As a young person and well into my adult life, I refused to share my opinion because that was something I just didn't do. If I said nothing then there wouldn't be any conflict. People who are there to guide you should show you the skills needed to cope with others. Instead, they displayed behaviors that I never want to exhibit. I grew up thinking, "Why am I so different?"

I knew from early on that I wanted to be a better person and not like those around me. Even in school, I wouldn't befriend those who chose to drink, smoke, or do drugs. The fear of being caught was always at the back of my mind, but thinking what God thought was in there somewhere. I remember sitting at my white desk trying to read my King James Bible. I wasn't a fast reader and I'm still not. Nor can I spell or write well. Knowing that, I'm not ashamed to say or share it. Could my lack of confidence be because I heard, "You're not going to make it in college?"

Words hurt, and sometimes they stay with us forever. You can't take back what you've said. You can say you're sorry but the damage is done. Bruises fade but all the words are stored in our memories. We react to situations too quickly with words and relationship building becomes difficult. You can forgive, but you never forget what was said.

My second mother-in-law said to me, "Don't listen to what he says or does. He doesn't really mean it."

What?

I still have a hard time understanding or even thinking that anyone should be allowed to act in that manner.

My fourth day on the trail started with a wake-up call from Corona Sam. He was standing at my tent at 4:30 a.m. trying to explain himself. Apparently, he had faced several tragedies in the past few weeks, and he was heavily burdened about those things that had taken place. He wanted to call off the hike but friends encouraged him to proceed.

I accepted his apology once again, but our relationship hasn't been reestablished. I thanked him for the invitation and opportunity to hike in Colorado, but he has "unfriended" me on Facebook. We shouldn't hold back when verbal hurts are thrown at us, but we need to contemplate how we will respond to them. I had rehearsed my speech for seven hours making sure that my words weren't hurtful in any way; however, I was going to be truthful.

My fourth day proved to be one of the most difficult ones. Emotionally and physically, it tested the core of who I am. I was concerned with Corona Sam's state of mind, and how I was going forward alone. The night before, I had entered Lost Creek Wilderness, which was established in 1980 and is made up of 119,790 acres of wilderness. I was going to ascend 1,100 feet before reaching almost 11,000 feet.

That doesn't seem like a lot of elevation gain, but as I started, I was at around 9,800 feet. I was breathing very heavily as I started my morning climb. My body started reacting to the altitude as I reached 10,000 feet. Stopping every 20-30 feet to breathe and sip on water (which helped), I crawled up the mountain. The book Altitude Illness: Prevention and Treatment states, "simply breathing more … is the most important factor." That sounds so easy. My resting pulse is around 46 but I still felt a pull on my heart as I climbed.

Later, when speaking with others about this first major climb, I learned that they had experienced some of the same afflictions. Apparently, those who urinate several times a night are likely to be more susceptible to altitude illness because you can lose up to two percent of your body weight in water. I was drinking more than three liters every day, and I'm one who uses the bathroom 2-3 times a night even at home. The other factor that affects people is the irregular sleeping pattern that is associated with altitude. Again, I'm not an individual who needs a lot of sleep, which can be helpful on the trail.

As I continued that day, I was reminded of the dense, cold forest of the Great Smoky Mountains National Park. I had only a brief moment to view the mountains in the distance. The sun came out, and I took a short break before the area was surrounded by fog. Those were cold days on my Appalachian Trail thru-hike in 2011. I just slowed my pace, and that worked for me. On this climb, I was averaging one mile per hour. I wasn't going to win a speed race, but I was moving forward.

Once I reached the top of this climb, I was blessed with all the colors of the rainbow in wild flowers that I found on the six-mile meadow hike along the North Fork Lost Creek. Every step I took, I saw another kind of flower. Even though it had rained heavily the night before, the blue bells were hanging on to life. Other flowers were popping up all around the meadow. I was hiking on the narrow path, and the sides were lined with flowers of every color. I stopped often to examine the clusters of flowers and take more pictures.

The sun was out, and I took the opportunity to stop and dry my gear. It had rained all night, and I had packed up a wet tent, which must have added five pounds to my pack weight. Placing all my wet gear in the sun, I decided to have a hot lunch. As I was packing up, the rain started.

Several hikers passed me. Stargazer, a mother of three whom I had met several times now, hiked with me for the remainder of the day. That afternoon, as we were sitting on

a long log, we started becoming cold and wanted to move forward to quickly reach the tree line, but the lightning started flashing overhead and the thunder sounded like clanging cymbals. With her head down, a young woman approached us, and we said, "Hi." She jumped, and her trail name was born - "Spook!"

The three of us stayed together during the lightning storm. We wanted to be sure that each of us was able to pass through the open areas safely. Upon reaching the tree line, Spook was gone. While stopping to take a picture at one spot called "the window," where the rocks formed a picture frame or window with the woods and snow-covered mountains in the distance as the subjects, I became very cold and needed to move quickly. My gloves, hat, and rain gear weren't keeping me warm. We took each other's picture, and I excused myself, moving down the mountain to warm my fingers and toes.

Entering Lost Creek Wilderness again, my hike for the end of the day would take me through an aspen/fir forest which has a root system that forms colonies that can live for thousands of years. I also enjoyed the Bristlecones - fine-needled pines that live in the poor soil of the high elevation areas. This variety of pine can live up to 5,000 years.

The rain stopped shortly before 6 p.m. and we decided to stop for the night. It turned out to be a 15-mile day. After treating some water and setting up my tent near a log that would deflect some water run-off during the night, I was ready to turn in for the night. It had been a pretty cold and wet day. I was missing Tom, and I prayed he was waiting for me at our first food drop, Kenosha Pass.

It rained during the night, and I wore my down jacket which made all the difference in getting a good night's sleep. I wasn't hungry the night before, so I made an effort to eat breakfast. I was packed and ready to hit the trail around 6:40

a.m. I had slept above 10,000 feet which made the hiking for this day much easier. I wasn't feeling my heart working as hard during this hike. My first food drop was coming up in about 11 miles. Stargazer was concerned that she didn't have enough food to reach Breckenridge if she slowed down any. I assured her that there would be plenty in my resupply, a supply of food and other items that would be needed.

Stargazer's knee was painful, and she was contemplating leaving the trail. I had felt my knees during my hike in the Smokies, and I remembered how much I had relied on my hiking poles. Leaning into them as I stepped down helped considerably. Sometimes I'm asked, "What is your favorite gear?" I never leave home without my hiking poles. When walking three miles on the road near my cabin, I use my poles. They save my knees and back and give my arms a workout as well.

As I passed an area covered in wild flowers, my nostrils were flooded with the sweet scent and the birds were going crazy. Was I too close to their nests? While hiking through a little mist, I heard the sounds of trucks. I really had been in

the wilderness for days. I reached Kenosha Pass well before noon. Only one hiker passed me that morning, and I was going to wait for Stargazer.

Much later, I listened to the recording I made on that hike into Kenosha Pass and heard my voice declaring my intentions with passion. "As mad as I can get about Tom, I know now why I am on this trail. Why we were separated. It's for me to find what I really want in life, and it is to love him and my family. I want to finish this trail, and be there to support my husband. It's something - that you can figure that out in five days on the trail. I want the beginning of a marriage on the Colorado Trail."

Days earlier, Tom had buried a food drop. I had seen the area roughly, but the exact spot was a mystery to me. Dropping my pack, I went in search of the orange five-gallon Home Depot bucket. I walked back and forth, but I couldn't see any ground that looked disturbed. I continued my search and nothing jumped out at me. First, I thought of why Tom wasn't there and then what I would do next. If I needed to resupply, Jefferson was only 4.5 miles south of Kenosha Pass.

Kenosha Pass was used by the Ute Indians and the white trappers who were heading to the South Park hunting grounds. During the gold rush in the mid-1800s, explorer John C. Fremont and other prospectors used this pass to travel to a dig around Fairplay. During the boom of the 1870s, trains serving Denver, South Park, and Pacific Railroad were running. Before the modern Highway was built in 1937, the pass became a toll road, and it was named after the hometown of Clark Herbert, a stagecoach driver.

I took a breather and prayed before walking back into the area. As I turned around, I looked to the left a few feet, and there I saw a plastic sandwich bag with a note. The one Corona Sam was going to leave for me. Under a branch, I found the bucket. No bear could get into that thing! Even using my poles and pulling with all that I had, it was a difficult job opening the bucket. After repacking my food, I ate and waited two hours for Stargazer. She never showed, but I met Ruth who planned on hiking section 4 a few weeks later. She was out training with her pack. I had passed her on my way into the parking area, and now she had returned from her hike.

We had a long chat. As she shared that she was going to be in a documentary because she had escaped a cult in her youth, I saw how I was conforming to things that didn't fit with my beliefs. We can be misguided at any age. It can be difficult to express your concerns and thoughts, but you have a right to be heard.

Ruth was willing to pick up the bucket the next day in order to "leave no trace." After leaving the remainder of the food for other hikers, I was ready to hike on.

I hiked along the railroad tracks, crossed the highway, and signed the log book at 2 p.m.

Three college girls were starting a day hike up the mountain. It was going to be around a 600-foot climb, and we

kept passing each other. I stopped to take a picture of the tepee-like structures, and they paused to remove their jackets. As I descended into the meadow, I had the clearest view of Georgia Pass and the Continental Divide in the distance. Finding a spot between the cow patties, I had a snack and gazed at the beauty that surrounded me. I was in a vast open area and not another soul was visible. I enjoyed those moments where it was just me and the world. No worries, just the here and now.

My goal was to hike to the bottom of the mountain. I wanted to start the six-mile ascent the next day. I hiked another three miles for a total of 55 miles in three days. Upon reaching my destination, I set up camp in a nice flat area. I pumped my water near the larger creek and then I was ready to crash. It had been a 17.7-mile day with food, views, and peace of mind. This turned out to be a second night without dinner. I had heard that altitude can affect your appetite. Eating is why I love to hike and I wasn't eating!

The best sleep. I found a flat place, and that's the key. It can be so difficult finding that just so spot. But I found it that night. After downing a protein shake and a breakfast bar, I was ready to tackle the almost 2,000-foot ascent over the next six miles. Tom and I had been apart for several days, and I was praying that he would find me. The best thing for me was to continue on the trail and let him find me there.

Having hiked several days alone, I was assured that I am who I am, and that I devote my all in any situation. I'm content with myself, and I'm unable to make others happy. Happiness and joy must be found within. It's important for individuals to figure out what's going on inside so they can deal with the outside issues.

I hiked a few miles and then, needing some protein, decided it was time for a second breakfast. I stopped and unpacked a few things. Nike, a thru-hiker from Denver, approached and I tried to invite him to eat some of my food. No go. I was carrying too much and not eating it. Two nights without dinner. You just don't feel hungry up there on the mountains. I was forcing myself to eat during the day so I could hike and I drank a recovery shake in the mornings to get a jump start. I just wasn't hungry in the evenings. Dinner was out as of now.

We spoke for a long time about hiking and how important it is to us. After finishing a pack of tuna with crackers, I was on my way again.

I thought that if only Tom would support me in completing this hike, I would be so ready to head home and be the wife he wanted. Sitting here writing that, I see now how he was slowly erasing my identity. I had married a man who had given so many years to American veterans' organizations, and he had turned into a manipulative individual. I can now see kind actions at the hairdresser's and the shop as acts of domination. He had to know my every move, and I became frustrated. His passive-aggressive moods happened every week. He would start an argument and act aggressive if I refused to engage in the discussion. He forced me to talk when I asked to be left alone. I needed time to reflect and process information, but that wasn't something he could allow. He couldn't wait until I was ready to communicate.

He had threatened to head home already, and at the time, I was shocked to hear those words. But it was another way to control the situation and have his way. I had asked, "Why?" No answer was forthcoming. I can only control my actions, thoughts, and feelings.

Coming out of the forest, I started seeing snow. It was July 9 and I had to take a selfie. Mount Guyot (pronounced gee-oh) was to the left of me. The sun was out and the sky was blue.

My first major mountain view was just ahead of me. As I approached the five-mile sign, I had a magnificent 360-degree view. The 14,000-foot mountains were still heavily covered with snow. People hike them and collect all kinds of patches. I have no desire to hike them. Hiking complete trails is my passion.

I was taking it all in, and I didn't want to rush this moment. I turned around several times, overwhelmed with the beauty of my surroundings. This moment in time was all mine. I realized that only I controlled my life, and I could be who I wanted to be.

There was a lot of activity on the summit. As I glanced up the trail, I saw a helicopter flying around and several people chatting. I continued to take pictures and then I noticed Nike speaking with the group. A four-wheeler was heading in that direction as well. Was someone being airlifted?

After taking a few more pictures, I started the final climb of the day that reached nearly 12,000 feet.

Several days before, Tom and I had finished our lunch by the emergency water supply, and that was the last time he saw me. He had a rough start to the hike, and his feet showed every mile. Since his feet weren't in the best of shape, he wasn't in a positive state of mind at times. The first day took a real toll on his feet. The hot sand cooked the soles of his feet, and since then, he had been playing catch up.

That day, he decided to hike to the store for some supplies because he had given me the stove and all the food. He didn't know where I had gone, and he needed a few things.

He knew we had talked about him resting his feet at the first food drop, but he felt sure he would catch up with me before nightfall.

He was not able to hitch a ride to the store, so he hiked miles on the road that didn't move him forward on the trail. Once he had bought a few things, he hiked back to the trail. The light was fading, and he found a cave to sleep in.

On the second day apart, he spoke with a police officer and he called Corona Sam's wife. Apparently, the officer was somewhat upset with the whole situation. Corona Sam had planned the hike but had not stayed with his hiking partners. Tom was given the itinerary, but had left it at home. After a lot of chatting, he found out that the hikers should have been camping in section 4 that night.

Hiking to the store a second time, Tom bought a cheap green tarp and headed out on the trail again. He hiked in the rain for several days. After sleeping at the Kenosha Pass Campground on July 8, Tom was ready to search again. He was sending messages via all the hikers that were passing him. It was the third day.

A young couple who were hiking with a dog realized that their dog wasn't able to hike the trail and decided to support their friends on the hike. They became Trail Angels - people who do kind things for hikers. On this day, they drove Tom around so that he could get in front of me.

Knowing that I had signed the register at 2 p.m. the day before, they figured I had hiked another 5-6 miles for the day, and would reach the summit of Georgia Pass that morning. Georgia Pass was another low area where the stagecoaches passed. The pass has become an obscure jeep track where hikers can park their cars to hike up to the summit.

Reaching the summit, he wrote a note on cardboard, "Meachele Mothership meet you in Breckenridge T. L. 9-10 July or when you get there. I'll be waiting there. Tom," and taped it to the sign that led down the mountain on the Colorado Trail, South.

A hiker approached the sign and Tom quickly asked him if he had seen his wife. "No, but you can see down the trail from over the ridge for miles." Tom went to where he could see down the mountain in the other direction, north, and there he saw a figure hiking towards them. He asked the hiker if he had seen "Mothership."

Nike informed him that he had just been chatting with me a few miles back. He had finally found me and now he waited as I hiked up the trail.

A man in an orange jacket was on the mountain. He was saying something, but I couldn't hear him. I said, "Pardon me." And then I realized that it was Tom. He had found me on July 9 at 10:30 a.m. atop Georgia Pass and the Continental Divide.

sharing

After taking several reunion pictures, we hiked down the jeep trail to pick up Tom's backpack. Upon meeting the couple who had helped Tom, I had a strong feeling of peace about them. And as we said thank you and goodbye, they handed me a card with their contact information.

It was a Good Samaritan Ministries card that said, "Good Samaritan Ministries has been performing simple acts of kindness in Brown County since 1993. We have been blessed by the generosity of churches, businesses and individuals. Through our hunger ministries, clothing store and financial assistance programs, we have blessed thousands of families through simple acts of kindness. In celebration of 20 years of blessings, we have commissioned 'Agents of Kindness' to go into the community to expand our reach through **Simple Acts of Kindness**. You too can join the celebration. Perform a simple act of kindness for someone. Leave this card behind and let's continue to bless our community one Simple Act of Kindness at a time."

Once we reached the summit again, we met Bends, who was hiking the trail for a few days. He was an Ultralighter, a hiker whose gear is around 10 pounds without food and water. He was wearing a Cuban Fiber skirt and his Cuban Fiber back-pack cover led me to believe that his pack weight was low. He asked if I was Mothership. Noticing the tattoo on my left ankle, which is composed of the Appalachian Trail symbol, my trail name, and the year I hiked, he was reassured that I was.

He informed us that the Kentucky father and two sons were leaving the trail. Erin, "Spook," had decided to doctor up and rest her feet, and Stargazer was heading home after reaching Breckenridge. Even this trail had people bailing out after a few days. Long distance hiking isn't always about the physical ability. The mental aspect plays a much greater role in accomplishing the task.

After the rundown on all the hikers behind us, we hiked on for a bit before breaking for lunch. I was able to offload some weight now that Tom was back, sharing the supplies. We had lunch in the sun, and Tom doctored up his feet. We descended to 10,000 feet that day. The two-mile drop with rocks and roots was tough. The rain set in and added to the difficulty.

We covered about eight miles and the rain didn't let up, so we decided to set up camp in the rain. That only made the already cold afternoon worse. Working fast, we were able to erect the tent without getting the inside wet. We retrieved the required supplies from our backpacks and left the wet gear outside. I covered my pack with my raincoat. After eating something cold for dinner, it was time to generate some heat.

It rained all night, but we stayed warm and dry in the tent. We heard the sounds of coyotes howling in the distance in the early hours of the morning. Up with the first birds, I went back to the creek and treated five liters of water. Tom was back at camp starting to dismantle the tent. Leaving camp around 7 a.m., I started hiking with cold fingers and toes. When we hit 11,000 feet, the temperature was around 35 degrees and the sun was starting to come out.

While hiking through a camping area, a biker informed us that the rain was coming around 2 p.m. At that point, rain came all the time. It was a fact of life during that first week. It could rain anytime during the day. The normal monsoon rainy season was changing its pattern. Just like people who change for the good or bad. We were hiking in an unusually wet season for Colorado.

The summit was cold and the flowers weren't visible until the descent. I had an eerie feeling that day as we continued on the path. It was cold and gloomy on that mountain. Not a sound was heard. Just two hikers following the trail down the mountain to Breckenridge.

On July 10, our hike would take us through a forest with areas of dead and dying trees as we entered the mountain village of Breckenridge. The mountain pine beetle, an insect native to the Colorado pine forests, is the size of a grain of rice and has a one-year life cycle. As of 2008, the pine beetle had killed some 2 million acres of forest. Large areas were cleared of dead trees, and they were stacked into piles.

Looking over the tops of dead or dying trees, we saw the vastness of the snow-covered mountain ranges that the Colorado Trail follows. This wilderness path crosses some of the most scenic areas of the Rockies and the Continental Divide. We were ready for a break and wanted to tend to our feet. Several days into the hike, I noticed that my right foot was giving me sharp pain that ran up my leg. The new insoles were working with my left foot but not the right one. This particular day, I decided to air out my insoles and as I started to place them back into my shoes, I noticed that they were two left insoles. No wonder my right foot was still hurting! The sales representative back home had given me the wrong one.

As we neared Breckenridge, we engaged in a lengthy conversation with a couple who had been visiting the area for the past 13 years. They said it was the wettest period they had ever seen. The alpine meadows and all the paths that led into towns were ornamented with the lush colors of wildflowers. The rain was stupendous for them. This area had fewer trees, but the wildflowers were impressive. My finger was trigger happy on the camera.

We had reached our first meaningful goal. We had hiked over 100 miles in seven days on the Colorado Trail. This trail leads over eight majestic mountain ranges, through six national forests, and along five river systems. Traversing these paths that usher you into civilization, you can't help but think about those people who passed here so many years ago.

The nomadic Ute Indians, who had wandered the mountains well before the first explorers set foot in the New World, were established by the 1600s in these mountain ranges. They combed the mountain territory as they followed the movement of game, partook in spiritual rituals, and conducted intermittent warfare with other tribes that infringed on their region. Even today, we travel on some of the paths that the Ute Indians did during their seasonal wandering.

The Summit Stage provided free bus service to several towns. So we headed to the first stop, a gas station, for some food and a cold drink. After recharging Tom's phone, we called the Fireside B&B to see if they had any availability for the night. Hearing the voice on the other end of the phone, I was ready for a day in town. They had a cancellation, and we took the room.

We also called Grizzle's brother Mark's phone and Corona Sam answered. He said that he had hiked extra miles and arrived yesterday. He obviously wasn't following the itinerary any longer because we had been to several of the planned stop sites with no Corona Sam. His agenda only. People like that aren't fun to be around, nor do I need them in my life.

After finishing our food, we walked to the bus stop once again to ride the three miles into Breckenridge. Long distance hikers love hiking the trails, but we aren't keen on hiking any extra miles to and from the trailheads. Upon reaching this charming mountain town, we navigated our way to 114 North French Street. The sun was out and the streets were filled with tourists.

Passing several people who looked like hikers, we climbed the hill to see the blue painted B&B on our right. We passed through several doorways and entered the low-ceilinged lounge. The walls were covered with relics from England. The owner took us through to the vaulted library that had a spiral staircase. We filled out our information and paid for the night which included a cooked breakfast and laundry.

After climbing the narrow flight of stairs, we were home for the night. It was a very large attic room with one double bed, four or five single beds, a small shower room, and a veranda with two chairs. I was able to dry our gear out on the veranda because the afternoon rain didn't come. After showering and delivering our soiled clothes to the laundry area, we decided to eat again.

Going as far as the lounge, Tom decided he wasn't able to walk any further that day. So we ordered a pizza which could have fed an army. It must have weighed 20 pounds! Half meat and half veggie. I had four meals from this pizza and that was after leaving four pieces for other hikers on the small communal table that served as an area for fixing meals. There was also a small white refrigerator and a wall-mounted individual storage area. This pizza was a feast! One of five meals in towns I would enjoy during this hike.

We ate, added pictures to Facebook, and called family. It was nice being inside, but the rain had finally let up and we were inside instead of on the trail. The day came to a close while we were hibernating in our room and planning the next day. Corona Sam was going to drop off our resupply at the B&B, and we wouldn't see him or Grizzle again.

Tom and I both needed to find some new shoes. Our shoes were too short for the steep descents. I had one toenail that had turned black already. When I had informed the shoe representative back home that I needed a half size larger, he hadn't considered the cork insoles, and hence, my shoes were too short.

Remembering how painful my feet were on the Appalachian Trail, I knew it would be difficult finding something that would work. I had hiked over 1,600 miles in Keen sandals and I knew that worked for me. But this time, I had decided to give closed shoes a try.

While sitting with several people at the larger dining room table, enjoying the conversation and the wonderful cooked breakfast, we checked to see if another night was available. No luck. Tom's feet needed a zero day - hiking no miles for the day. Leaving our backpacks at the B&B, we headed into town.

Breckenridge is a restored mining/railroad town that is the center of the Summit County resort area. All sorts of people practice their hiking, climbing, and mountain biking skills in the summer, and the area offers a multitude of winter sports to be enjoyed.

Our first stop was the post office because Tom was sending home a few items. Once you're out a week, you can start narrowing down the things that aren't needed. It's a great idea to lighten your load. I feel so much lighter emotionally when I'm out hiking a long distance. Daily stress is about the necessities: food, water, and shelter. And everything else you leave at home. Our food would be at the B&B shortly, the two-man tent was working out great, and the water supplies were manageable. The gear was working out. We just needed to replace our shoes.

Tom found a pair of trail shoes that worked for him, and after checking all the shoe shops, I returned to the first place we had looked and bought another pair of Keen sandals. Since I was unable to locate a pair of men's, I settled for a women's pair. We enjoyed the shops and all the activity that the main street offered.

Our shopping spree ended around 2 p.m. and it was time to check to see if our resupply had been dropped off at the

B&B. We were ready to repack our food. Repacking allows us to cut weight, and we're able to recycle the boxes. Once everything was accounted for, we added any unnecessary extra supplies to the hiker box. A hiker box is where individuals donate anything they aren't using, such as food, toilet paper, lotion, fuel, and so much more. We added my shoes, extra food, and toilet paper.

Loaded up, we traveled on the bus to the Wayside Inn where we spent the night. Not the wonderful B&B but clean. Tom feel asleep rather quickly, and I watched TV for a few hours. I was getting anxious about hitting the trail again. Several hikers were going to slack pack, or hike with a smaller backpack for the day, the section into Copper Mountain. Not only were they slack packing, but they were going to take the bus to Copper Mountain and hike back to Breckenridge. Hiking in that direction, they would have only a four-mile climb, whereas we were going to have an eight-mile climb with all our gear and a fresh resupply. Must say I didn't think that one through.

Breckenridge is a wonderful historical mining town that is filled with shops and activities near the river for all to enjoy. It's a super clean town with small museums and anything your heart desires can be found there. I was sorry to leave this place of both natural and man-made beauty.

On July 12, I had a cup of coffee and the last slice of pizza, and we were off at 9 a.m. A beautiful, sunny, warm day greeted us as we crossed the highway and started our climb from the Gold Hill Trailhead. It was a Sunday morning, and the trails were busy with hikers and mountain bikers. It was slow going through the burnt logging area. The markers were hard to spot, and Tom was breaking in his new shoes. As we gazed up the trail, we saw a cloud that had formed just above the mountain. It looked like the saucer-shaped cloud was part of the mountain. When we reached the two-mile mark, we would head down for a mile and then the long five-

mile climb would be upon us. Stopping near a small creek, we shared the trail with mountain bikers as they whizzed by.

It was time to eat something in order to lighten the load. My pack was every bit of 30 pounds on this leg of the trail. I became very purposeful with what I ate during the day. I ate protein in the mornings and the evenings and higher calorie items during the day. It seemed to work. I was hiking the miles, but my speed wasn't there.

Finding some lush green grass, we took another break in the sun. I closed my eyes and could have napped all afternoon in the sun. Moving on, we were still heading down and wondered why we weren't climbing yet. We saw more day hikers out and began to question our whereabouts. When we finally arrived at a fork in the trail, I knew that we had missed a marker. We were on a side trail that lead into Frisco.

Our detour added five miles to the hike, but it was nice seeing the miner's cabin on the Miner Rd., and I enjoyed the warm sunny day. I wasn't in a rush to be in the cold that waited for us on the 12,000-foot mountain. The rundown miner's cabin was about 8 by 12 feet and the door was only about five feet tall. Once back on the Colorado Trail, we stopped between two nice-sized creeks. We had hiked 10 plus miles but only 4.8 miles on the CT. After setting up the tent on a slight incline, I ambled to the creek and treated 7.5 liters of water. The sun was still out, so I washed myself and some clothes. Tom cooked the eight-serving bean soup. We ate every bite and also downed some trail mix. Enjoying the warm evening, we stayed outside for a long while.

I couldn't sleep. So, I sat on the old wooden bridge that crossed the second creek near our camp site. I listened to the night and watched the clouds roll across the sky. The water rushing over rocks drowned out any other noises in the forest. It was a dry night, and I was content to sit there for hours. This was entertainment for me; simply hiking the trail, sitting in the dark, and seeking simple pleasures.

Waking Tom up at 5:30 a.m. wasn't easy because he wanted to stay in the cozy sleeping bag. After finishing our hot breakfast, we started hiking around 6:20 a.m. I saw a bit of red in the sky, but didn't know what kind of day we were going to have. We were just going walking in the woods. This was a straight up kind of trail. There were seasonal runoffs that still had ample water. We could have filled up further up the mountain, but didn't want to take a chance on finding water. This season water proved to be plentiful.

We had broken up the 3,600-foot climb into two days and would be above the tree line for the first time. Shortly before leaving the trees, a thru-hiker named Caveman, who had a gold tooth on the right side, stopped for a quick chat. He

liked Tom's kilt and decided to name Tom "Scotsman." That's how he received his trail name.

Passing through a magical valley filled with rock formations and eerie-looking trees that resembled the talking trees in the "Lord of the Rings" movies, we eventually stepped onto a narrow path that blocked the wind. We continued to relish the warm mid-morning weather. Putting one foot in front of the other on this path was difficult if you wanted to appreciate the views. Tom spotted two elk in the tree line below. I could spot only stationary objects that were relatively close!

After watching the elk, he wanted some jerky. His eyes lit up as he realized that I had bought him a pack of elk jerky in Breckenridge. A biker was pushing his bike and navigating the narrow path through the brush. He stopped and chatted a bit. It's a small world! His daughter goes to Appalachian State University in Boone, NC. He said, "I love that area." Since he had no camera, I offered to take several pictures that he could pick up in the fall. Now back to the jerky. The biker was standing there and Tom never offered him any. We ate the whole pack as we were chatting. Well, bikers can get into town much faster than hikers. But it's still polite to offer.

We reached the tundra and had a perfect day cresting the Tenmile Range. The cumulus clouds had been forming all afternoon, but no precipitation materialized as we crossed the ridge. Snow drifts were still visible, but the snow was melting rapidly. Having a clear view of Breckenridge to the east, Dillon to the north, and the large watershed, Lake Dillon, was an added bonus since we had experienced so much rain during the first week of hiking. The wildflowers continued to capture my attention. Words can't describe the elegance displayed by these delicate flowers. Full of grace and so fragile-looking, yet they can withstand monsoons that hit them. I would like to stand strong, like the wildflowers, and withstand the storms of life, bouncing back as they do.

The alpine tundra is similar to a desert because the steep mountains receive little precipitation. The snow is blown away by the fierce winds and the thaw runs off quickly. The wildflowers and other vegetation rely on the sum-

mertime afternoon thunderstorms for their survival. The sweet-smelling alpine forget-me-nots embedded in the rock crevices are one such wildflower. As the Colorado Trail winds its way through forests, meadows with river beds, tundra, boulder fields, mesa areas, and mountaintops with permanent ponds, you encounter thousands of flowering plant species.

Life zones are defined by the elevation, the ecosystem, and the plants that inhabit the area. The following are five life zones and their elevations: plains (3,500-6,000 feet), foothills (6,000-8,000 feet), montane (8,000-10,000 feet), sub-alpine (10,000-11,500 feet), and alpine (11,500-14,400 feet).

As we drew near the boulders and the six foot high snow-field, a pika greeted us with his piercing bark. He ran back and forth to get our attention. It seemed as though he had been fed in the past. He knew what hikers were about. Taking turns sitting on the rocks, we took pictures in all directions and of our cute new friend, the pika.

As we crossed over the top, we were fully exposed and the wind picked up. I was developing a headache. Was it because we were nearing 12,500 feet or due to the eight ounce cup of coffee I had yesterday? First cup in ten days. I think it was the elevation. The coffee was too weak to affect me. I stopped to retrieve my yellow wind breaker and drink some water.

The barren mountaintop, which had minimal vegetation, offered views in all directions. They were magnificent, but I was becoming cold. Picking up my pace on the rocky path, I was prepared for the steep descent which would lead me to the tree line below. After reaching the cover of some trees, we decided to munch once again. Long distance hikers burn between 4,000-6,000 calories a day. It seems as though we're consuming food all day long.

As the sun continued to radiate brightly in the sky, I relaxed and dozed for a spell. It felt as though we were on a picnic with the lush green grass under us and our stomachs satisfied for the time being. When we felt the first raindrops of the day, it was time to move on. I fetched my rain jacket, keen on reaching Copper Mountain Resort.

In another two miles, we would navigate our way around another resort. On the Wheeler Trail, we passed two trail crews, many of whom are volunteer trail maintenance crew members from all over, and were invited to visit with other crew members who had stayed behind in the large communal tent at the trailhead. As we proceeded to the tent which was erected in the parking lot, the summer sky suddenly turned dark and threatening. We talked for a while with a French couple who had passed us on the trail and two crew members. Conversation topics included: Where are you from? Why are you hiking the trail? How much is your pack weight? The same questions seem to come up on shorter trails as on longer ones. Since it is a shorter trail, bonds aren't formed as easily. When you're hiking for four to six months, as is the custom on the Appalachian Trail, you develop a kindred spirit with other thru-hikers. You share so much more than on a 36-day trek.

Evening was near and we arranged for our packs to remain at the trail crew tent while we traveled to Frisco on free transportation. Arriving shortly before the persistent downpour, we strolled around the shopping center and entered the food court. Feeling the cold in my bones, I wanted something hot to dine on. A hot bar was just the thing. It was time to partake of some needed calories. A six-piece chicken dinner with all the fixings, a jumbo cup of soup, and a broccoli salad were up for grabs. We paid, then sat near the window and watched the rain flood the parking area as we devoured everything on the table.

We purchased three more meals and discussed the possibility of hiking more slowly. Tom required more time to recover and tend to his feet. Since our first zero day, we'd hiked only 18 miles. The precipitation let up briefly and gave us a short window to catch the last bus back to Copper Mountain Resort. There was no camping allowed for the next four miles near the resort, so we asked the crew director if we could camp near their campsite. The French couple was staying there for the night as well. The temperature dropped, and the rain subsided. I found a spot and moved swiftly to pitch our tent.

The unrelenting downpours lasted throughout the night. We slept in and started the day around 9 a.m. The trail crew had gathered their tools and were at their work stations before we had packed up. Navigating around the Copper Mountain Resort, we were close to the apartments and condos. The trail passed under the ski lifts. We saw mountain bikers riding the lifts and coming down the slopes into the resort, and we headed into the center. This area wasn't anything like Breckenridge. It was rather dead. If it wasn't for the mountain bikers and hikers, the place would be deserted. After sharing a second breakfast, it was time to tackle the next mountain.

The hike on the day before had included a rough vertical climb filled with roots and rocks. This ascent proved to be extremely pleasant. The trail was shared by bikers, hikers, and horseback riders. Although we were scaling another mountain, it became the enchanted forest. Once we had passed the resort, the area was surrounded by dense woods until we reached Guller Creek. A local biker conveyed his passion for this valley. He said, "This is the most attractive area on the Colorado Trail!"

The sky was showing signs of yet another thunderstorm. The guidebook was very clear and stated, "Summer thunderstorms can move in quickly and catch people off guard." We heard the rumbling and started thinking about our next move. In life we can be caught off guard as well. And what do we do then?

On this occasion, several large and beautiful trees would shelter us from the determined and turbulent storm. Some of the spruce-fir forests are 400 years old, and the very dense tree clusters can provide a refuge for hikers. The rain started as we were pitching the tent between two trees just a few feet away from the creek. Sitting under the immense branches, we were able to cook dinner and remain dry. We had hiked only 5.2 miles, but this was the enchanted forest

and the pixies were calling for us to stay. After enjoying a hot meal, it was time to sort out the sleeping arrangements. I dozed in and out that night. But I did see stars for the first time. Did this mean that we were going to have some better weather?

I try to recall any conversations between Tom and me since our reunion at Georgia Pass. None come to mind. Why is that? This was an adventure we were supposed to share together, but somehow that wasn't happening.

Waking up to the roar of the river, we were eager for the silence the trail provided. Our ears were ringing with the noise of the water flowing. The river had swelled with the massive amount of rain that had fallen during the night. The sun was showing itself, but it was a jacket and glove kind of day. While ascending through the dense forest for several more miles, I felt the chill. The sun was climbing in the sky, and no rain was visible for the moment. Before exiting this glorious green-carpeted narrow valley, we ambled slowly up the trail with the sound of Guller Creek's abundant water flow resonating off the cliffs.

Through the forests, we used the double-peaked triangular logo of the official Colorado Trail sign on posts and trees as our guide, but now we were seeing many more rock cairns - man-made heaps or stacks of stones which are used as landmarks in the tundra. Some of the cairns were works of art. On misty days, they can be seen from a distance and reassure hikers that they are on the trail. We glanced down the valley for the last time as we saw the cairn that marked the next turn that ascended to Searle Pass. At the pass, we stopped to eat a protein bar and some beef jerky because our bodies had used up our small breakfast.

We were in the open and clouds were forming, so I began to pray. There was no place to find shelter from a raging storm. But the Lord was watching over us that day. The clouds continued to form and moved out of our area. Across the vast tundra, we marched on the very narrow path without stopping. How the wildflowers survive the monsoons and the cooler evening temperatures is a mystery to me. With

only 30-40 frost-free days and sometimes less than 20 inches of precipitation a year, the cushion plants have a harsh environment, yet they display impressive colors during their short season of growth. It takes some plants a century to produce a mat one foot in diameter.

While scanning for the next marker, we continued to climb even on the tundra. The markers weren't very noticeable from a distance but once we were on the climb it was a different story. With the wind whipping through both passes, we didn't stop much. We reached the oversized sign for Kokomo Pass sign captured the historic moment on film. Three hours later, we stopped for a late lunch. We had reached the tree line and the sun was still out.

After drying the tent, we hiked on for another mile or so. Finding a nice site with water was the key, and as we rounded the trail, we saw the perfect place. The site was a designated campsite with three trees, a fire pit, a flat spot, and water. After we had the tent set up, it started to spit rain a bit. I climbed down a 15 foot embankment to fill our water bottles. It was a cooler evening so I just soaked my feet before returning to the campsite. Hiker mid-night, 9 p.m., had arrived, and I found delight in the sunset. My mother always said, "Red sky at night, sailors delight. Red sky in the morning, sailors take warning."

The next morning was much cooler, and I knew Tom was in some pain. The plants all had a soft white covering on them. The temperature was in the mid-30s and it felt much colder in the valleys.

Tom was rapidly descending into the "poor me mood." I would say something to help him, and he would twist my words, and make me appear to be the bad one; the uncaring, selfish individual who only thinks of herself. And then he would tell me not to listen to the words that came out of his mouth. How could I not? They hurt.

I was wearing two jackets as we headed down the trail that was covered in a light frost. My fingers and toes were numb. A second group of trail workers were waking from their slumber as we passed by. Ahead of us the mountains were in clear view and they were cloaked in white. Was this the Mount of the Holy Cross? W. H. Jackson's photo had captured the image of a massive snowy cross which was established as a national monument in 1929. That status was rescinded shortly after World War II, but the place could still be a place of faith healing because anything is possible with God.

Mountain of the Holy Cross, Colorado, by William Henry Jackson - Department of the Interior. General Land Office. U.S. Geological and Geographic Survey of the Territories. (1874 - 06/30/1879)

nightmare

"And have no fellowship with the unfruitful works of darkness, but rather expose them."

Ephesians 5:11

As I continue my walk with the Lord, I'm reminded that we are to show love whenever possible but also withdraw ourselves from immoral people who call themselves Christians. This process is redemptive and not punitive. The goal is that the Christian will ask for forgiveness and once again obey God's word. It's a heart thing and what joy you can experience when you know Him! Only then will you have peace, joy, and happiness.

The next valley was set up as a training camp in 1942. Camp Hale used the flat valley and surrounding steep hillsides as an area to teach skiing, rock climbing, and winter survival skills. In the early 1960s, it was used by the CIA to train Tibetan rebels. Aged concrete bunkers are visible on this valley floor. Just as soldiers in the past stood at attention, the beautiful yellow sunflowers hold their ground as they face the sun. And we can withstand the battles in this world when we look to the Bible for guidance.

As we marched on, it became ever so difficult to motivate Tom. Being able to stand in the sunshine was motivation enough for me. The sun was over the mountaintops and hitting my back. It felt so nice walking in the open on that cool morning. He had thrown down his pack for a second time and still gave no response about what he wanted to do. Was this a temper tantrum? We had hiked about eight miles of an easier section of the Colorado Trail. We stopped at around 11 a.m. so that Tom could rest for the day and see what the following day brought.

It was a long day in the tent. I slept on and off. The sun was bright with only a few light showers. If we hiked 11.3 miles a day, we could finish the Colorado Trail in 30 more days. That is a comfortable amount of miles per day, but I wasn't getting any input from Tom. The sun finally went down and I waited for daylight.

The morning was cold, and I packed up quickly in order to get my body moving. Crossing the road, we were in the valley with no sun. The valleys are so cold. My knees and fingers were so cold. We raced across the valley to reach the sunny area.

My journal entry for that morning states, "Racing through the partially dense forest to reach the first beam of sunlight, but the clouds took it away. So, our numb bodies are still pushing forward to see if we can get that first sunshine onto our bodies to thaw us out."

We passed several ant mounds which ranged in size from a foot to several feet in circumference, but the ants were not showing themselves that morning. The valley was quiet and cold. And only two hikers were passing through the area. As the sun climbed into the sky and over the mountaintops, I stopped and let the sun's rays hit me for a few minutes before the clouds blocked the warmth once again. I continued to wiggle my toes and fingers to get some circulation going. As we followed the narrow path through the valley, the tall grass hit my knees and kept them from warming up. I walked faster and hoped that it would be warmer in a few hours.

Life's valleys can be cold as well, but with prayer and help we can overcome many obstacles. An individual must desire to change and practice change. As youngsters we're told, "Practice makes perfect." And that continues throughout our lives. Are you a willing vessel?

I picked up my pace because Tom was in such a negative mood. He kept saying things like, "If the train still ran, I would lay on the tracks," or "I'm going to slice my throat." I didn't know if I should take these as suicide threats or if he was trying to get a reaction out of me. He wanted to start a fight, and I was quiet. I was not going to be roped into that negative behavior.

The path leading up to the oven ruins were beautiful. It was like a carriage trail. It was an easy walk through the forest and I could smell the scent of freshly washed clothes. The cold air brings smells to life.

We passed the ruins of two ovens which were used to produce high-grade "coke" for steel. Coming into Tennessee Pass, the parking lot was busy with excited Boy Scouts going on a backpacking trip. Tom spoke with a scout leader in such a positive tone, like everything was great, and I used

the bathroom. His mood swings were so drastic. Happy and wonderful with a stranger who was a man, and in an instant, he would change like "Dr. Jekyll and Mr. Hyde." Leaving the company of enthusiastic hikers, we headed into the woods. It was a gentle walk at 10,424 feet. Our bodies were doing fine at this altitude.

Tom said, "I'm hungry. We need to stop."

"Ok, there is a bench and a swing. We could stop there." I replied.

He took off his backpack and threw the one gallon plastic bag full of cereal bars at me. I told him that I had taken two out that morning before leaving camp. As soon as I handed him the bag, he asked if I was ready to go.

"Have you eaten yet?" I questioned.

"No, I took some pills," he answered.

Then it happened. He stood in front of me as I was putting my backpack on.

"I'm your husband and you're going to respect me," he stated.

He proceeded to pull my hair, knock my glasses off, and threaten to break my hiking poles, and then pushed me to the ground. This all happened so fast that I was in shock and didn't really know what to do. I remember being very still for a few minutes and then I shouted a few times. While I was on the ground, he leaned across me from the left to the right and bit my right thigh. At that point, I noticed my hiking poles next to him. I reached for them and stuck him in the stomach with them. This gave me a chance to undo my backpack and run back to the parking lot. At that stage, I didn't realize he had taken his neck knife out and cut the load straps on my backpack.

I knew I could reach the safety of the parking lot before him. Once I got there, a young gentleman and his lady friend were kind enough to drive me to the nearest phone. As we were turning around, Tom came out of the woods saying, "Meachele, let's go to town and fix your backpack."

As we headed for the ski resort, the young man asked me, "Are you sure you want to call the police?" Hello! My husband just attacked me! If it were anyone else, you would be calling the police. Why wouldn't I? Just because he's my husband doesn't give him the right to physically abuse me. He lost control and would have to deal with the consequences.

The young man knew that there was an emergency phone at the ski resort. I opened the wooden box that held the phone and all of the emergency numbers were written out on the door. Tom had walked up to the ski hut and wanted to talk with me. At a distance, he starting saying something, but the sheriff arrived within a few minutes. He escorted Tom to the patrol car and then asked for my statement. The police officer asked if Tom had any weapons. I told him that he had two knives. Tom had given up only one knife and was told that it would be a felony charge if deputies had to retrieve the other knife. Tom told him where to find the other knife, which was the one he had used to cut my backpack straps.

The officer stated that the knife looked pretty old and beat up, but it was a new knife. Did Tom know what he was doing?

After all this, the officer asked me, "What would you like to do?"

I knew that a restraining order was in place, but I still wanted to get some distance between us. My response was, "Go hiking."

"With a messed up backpack?" he said.

"I'll figure something out," I answered.

darkness

Why is it that people refuse to listen when you're sharing your story? At 56 years of age, I'm at a point in my life where I'm not going to be a victim any longer. My mind wants to "Be Free" of past abuses. Freedom is what I seek.

Beth Moore's book, *When Godly People Do Ungodly Things*, states, "Remember, we're talking about godly people with wholehearted devotion who were seduced. None of us is ever sinless, but these people were not living under the dominion of any sin when they were attacked. No, sin is not where the enemy most often gets his foothold on the godly. Rather, we're about to see, where this kind of victim is concerned, the enemy more often latches on to weakness, or maybe I should say a hidden spot of vulnerability... Satan knows that weakness can turn to sin in a heartbeat when exposed to just the right amount of pressure."

Today, I finally shared many past events with my mother, and she could only start commenting on her childhood and the time she left my father for a year. This was about me. Couldn't you just be a mother and listen? It always ends up about her. Is that why I never shared the sexual abuse that took place at the age of 6 or 7? Or the date rape that took place so many years ago? Would she have believed it or come up with some kind of reason why it didn't happen?

It was a family friend and everyone respected him. How could anything like that occur in a small German town? Even today she said, "We lived in a room in a guest house in Germany, and I had to work from morning to night to have food for us." Okay, she had it hard as well, but I was expressing myself.

Just last week, my son and I were in a counseling session, and the counselor kept looking at the door as people passed by. Is there anyone out there who wants to hear the victim's story?

Since my first husband passed away, I'm living in two families. My two older sons love the ground their father walked on, and my youngest son hates everything about his father. If there were a stronger word for "hate," I would use it here.

I was told many years ago that he had a dark side. After being told that he possibly had sexually abused my friend's daughter, I confronted my husband, and he assured me that nothing had happened. Both of those conversations have been at the back of my mind for a very long time. Had I heeded the warning or had he been charged with that offense, other abuses and hurts could have been prevented. The guilt and shame is eating me up now. What could I have done differently?

Raising three boys, I read all I could to bring them up in a loving, caring, and protective environment. The book *Bringing up Boys* by Dr. Dobson became one I reviewed often. I had firsthand experience in the sexual abuse arena, and I wanted my boys to be free from any harm. Little did I know that something was happening under my roof, and I had no knowledge of it. How could I have been so blind?

Fast forward to the time we decided to adopt two troubled brothers. I heard something that didn't sit right with me, and I let the counselor know. I was told that they had a lot of built-up anger about their biological father, so it wasn't uncommon for them to say things about the other males in their life. Life went on.

Then one day, I saw something that looked out of place, and I was pretty upset. Again, I confronted my husband and he brushed the situation off. I was not feeling at peace, so I took the two younger boys to my mom's home in Chapel Hill, NC. Two of the other boys were on a trip with friends, and the oldest was working.

I returned the following day, and I told the police everything that I knew. They stated that this would be reported to Department of Social Services. They asked if I was okay with it. And I said, "Yes." Once again, my biological sons and my two adopted sons were asked questions. Everything was cleared again. How can this be?

Was I dreaming things up and wanting something to be there when nothing was?

In September 2006, just as the new school year was starting, another allegation was reported - against me this time. DSS came to our cabin and started asking questions about our morning routine. We lived in a 950 square foot cabin, and seven people were living there at the time. Everything could be heard in the small area. So, nothing happened that morning. The boys wanted to leave, and I was disappointed, but it was the best for them.

A year later, Ray was charged with several counts of sexual abuse. He went to the grave stating that he was innocent. The lawyer asked me if I was ready to testify for my husband. I remember saying, "My heart says he didn't do anything, but my mind says otherwise." I still don't know what took place, but the victims know everything. And now it's time for them to find the freedom they deserve.

I know how guilt and shame dominates the very core of who you are. You carry that with you for days, months, and years.

You don't share anything with others because they aren't going to believe you, or you think it was your fault, or the abuser promises never to act that way again, or threatens you. Any combination of these can be the reason why we, the victims, aren't able or willing to share our hurts and concerns.

As youngsters, we're told to obey our elders, and as adults, we become too ashamed to share any past hurts because we don't want people to feel sorry for us. I'm strong. I was able to deal with sexual abuse and much more. I don't want anyone looking at me differently because I went through difficult situations. I don't need their pity. It would be nice to chat with others that have been through this.

Being a person who takes the time to listen and encourage those that have seen abuse or been abused goes a long way. The road to recovery from such a childhood trauma can take years. I was blessed that the Lord was always close as I went through sexual, verbal, and physical abuse. He was also the one I ran to during those times of recovery.

On October 8, 2015, my son went for his first counseling session and as he started to follow the counselor up the hall he turned and said, "Mom, since Dad is dead, can I talk about anything?" I just wanted to cry. He sounded like a child of eleven asking for permission to speak. His dad has been dead five years and still has a hold on him. How could anyone demand a child to keep a secret? It's our responsibility to listen and if you feel that something isn't right, question, question, and find out what's going on. I'm eaten up with guilt and shame because I wasn't there to protect my son and because of what happened. If only I could turn back the clock, I might be able to prevent all the heartaches and lost childhood years. I want to cry, scream, and even kill the man who's already dead. But I looked at my son and said, "You talk about anything and everything." God, I want him healed and all the others healed who may have suffered.

recovery

In our society, there is still some stigma associated with abuse and the recovery that victims are going through. It's like we see them as plagues. If we get too close, we may catch something. I've found that I'm honored to be in the presence of a victim who is in recovery because they are learning compassion and love that's beyond anything I've seen. They care for one another and show it so openly. Their feelings and thoughts are shared without judgment or others becoming defensive.

After what occurred at Tennessee Pass, I was once again faced with my own recovery. How was I going to process this latest event? My husband thought it was necessary to put his hands on me. And now as I'm sitting at home writing this story, I'm dealing with another major meltdown. I'm saddened that this physical abuse took place: two sons love the ground their dad walked on, while one son has held in 14 years of hurt and is walking through recovery in a positive way. And then there are those around us who haven't a clue or desire to be part of the process. Is it that they are reluctant to see what has taken place in the past? Or unable to forgive the victim's actions, even though they know what the victims went through? Words are cheap. Show me that you care. What are you willing to do? Continuing to live in fear and not allowing present positive actions to speak for themselves is mind boggling.

We give up on people. Yet we have past and present issues that need to be handled. We aren't without blemishes. Change is possible and we must be part of that or remove ourselves for their well-being. Allow them to have loving, caring, listening individuals in their lives. It humbles me when others can forgive. Being able to forget and move forward in the relationship is the key to peace and happiness.

Processing through the hurts takes time, and that's something that I struggle with. Recovery isn't something you do alone, and as a society, we need to open our hearts. Take the time to be there for the victims. Make an effort to help that individual on the road to a happier and healthier life. Can you listen and encourage others? Stop isolating people because they are victims of what someone else did. The victims didn't ask to be abused and yet we allow them

to suffer alone. I must learn to let go of those who aren't willing to be part of the healing process.

"God, grant me the serenity to accept the things I cannot change; the courage to change the things I can; and the wisdom to know the difference."

-Reinhold Niebuhr

paradise

As I hiked back to the Tennessee Pass parking lot, I was totally alone. My husband had been arrested for assaulting me just an hour earlier, and now I was hiking the remainder of the Colorado Trail on my own. How was I going to handle this new life that was before me? In the past, I believed that God wants you to work out everything, but the more I prayed, I could see only what God says about treating your wife as He treats the church. Neither a husband nor anyone else has the right to abuse me or anyone else. Living in fear isn't what I wanted.

After passing through the winter resort area where the 10th Mountain Hut System, a nonprofit group formed in 1980, linked several huts together so that experienced backcountry travelers could find rustic accommodation and explore the 300-mile trails, I approached the Holy Cross Wilderness Area. It was the perfect name for an area that would show me God's face. Entering the valley with a stream running on the left side, I felt as if I was transported to heaven. The six plus miles since leaving the Pass had been extremely difficult for me. I was shocked and angry with what had just taken place. And now I was alone again. Why were these things happening to me? I try so hard to make others happy that I lose my own identity. It's like they want to turn me into something I'm not.

In my own family, individuals would say things like; "Nana Meachele, you're too happy." Or "You're not a real grandma because you're not home baking cookies." I can never be too happy and I'm a grandma who likes to hike long distances and ride horses! Why is that so hard to understand or accept?

I gazed at the wooden sign and then entered paradise, the Holy Cross Wilderness area. Within this area, I had a restful stop near the river's edge. I decided to soak my hot feet in the cold, fast-flowing water. A large stone was submerged at the bank. It was the perfect place to collect water and bathe my feet. The sun was shining, and I had all the time in the world to

take a break. It didn't take long for me to drop my backpack and have my socks and shoes off.

My feet were throbbing as the fresh mountain water made its way past my lower extremities. After some time, I laid myself down in the thick, lush, green grass that was so inviting. I could have easily stayed in that hidden valley which had become my refuge for that afternoon. At that moment, I was at peace. The sun was warm on my body, my feet enjoyed the rest, and I felt God was protecting me.

After a long rest period, I hiked another five miles. Climbing some 500 feet, I was on narrow paths which were traveled by horses. I couldn't believe that people would bring horses on

these paths. It was a difficult climb up to the saddle of Porcupine Lakes. In the 1930s, the Civilian Conservation Corps built the old Main Range Trail which served as recreation and fire protection. I had views of the granite formations, and the fact that I was in the Rockies was becoming a reality that afternoon.

With the lakes on the summit, one could easily escape the world and find a tranquil place to call home on this mountaintop. As I was taking pictures of the rugged mountain range that was slightly covered with the last snow, the silence was broken as a young woman with her bear bell passed me very quickly. I was astonished that someone could pass this amazing view without taking a few moments to savor this peaceful place.

On this last five-mile section, I indulged in several breaks that weren't necessary. The saddle was covered with boulders and lush green grass. The evergreens were full and

green. The wildflowers were a carpet among the rocks that covered the area. The small, fluffy white clouds were passing by. A friend described me to another person as, "The individual who goes around a corner and always finds something beautiful." And that's how that afternoon turned out to be. I had hiked through gentle, rolling wooded footpaths which led into a valley flowing with sweet water, to several climbs that opened to a flat summit with water and glorious views. Around every corner there was something else to admire and I thanked God for allowing me to see this place that day. It was paradise for me.

rocky

The peacefulness surrounding Holy Cross Wilderness Area was very short-lived. The sun was still high in the sky and the weather was dry. So, I continued hiking and left this spot which has a special place in my heart. It was a refuge for me during my time of need, but I had to face the days ahead.

I ambled on until my feet could go no further. I had enough water, so I wasn't looking for a campsite with water. It would be safer for me to find a campsite off the trail. Jumping to the left of the trail, I started scouting for a suitable place to pitch my tent. There were so many small rocks beneath the surface of the ground. It would be impossible to find the perfect place that night, but I was exhausted from the events of the day and hiking 14.7 miles with three climbs.

Shortly before dark, I crawled into my tent. I was running low on food and can't remember if I ate anything that evening. It was a very restless night, and my heart was beating faster than normal. Was this due to the altitude or the incident at Tennessee Pass? I jumped every time I heard a noise in the woods.

The following day started off difficult and remained that way throughout the day. But first, I passed the Boy Scout troop who had started from Tennessee Pass. They were still in deep slumber as I ambled by their campsite. I would have slept better if I knew of their presence. And then I came upon the still lake that calmed my soul. Shortly thereafter, I was in the area which was covered in boulders and it was very dry. Since my pain medication was removed from my backpack in Tennessee Pass, I felt everything. My feet and back were screaming at times. This was such a day! While descending a series of steep switchbacks and maneuvering my body across large boulders, I could feel every muscle working overtime. I was in the Rockies.

Starting section 10, I came across a young woman whom I had met the day before. She was out for a few days and her father met her each evening at a designated place. They were just packing up and offered me some coffee. Breakfast was over and I realized I must have started hiking quite early that morning. While I was taking a short break, a fifth female solo hiker passed me. I have seen more female hikers on the trail since the book and movie Wild hit the shelves.

Entering the Mount Massive Wilderness Area, I registered and filled in the dates I would be camping in the area. Without a watch or phone, I never knew what time it was. I ate two packs of tuna and several crackers and hoped to have some energy. A day hiker had just informed me that it was only 12:30 p.m. and I had hiked over 8 miles already. I was so tired and there were several more "ups" to go on this section. I met several more females out hiking the trail, and we would leapfrog each other for the next few days.

My body was drained of energy and after several more breaks, I finally called it a day. Two other hikers had hoped to reach the North Willow Creek campsite, but they stopped a few miles short of that destination. And I had gone an extra mile. Finishing the day with just over 12 miles, I was whipped. My body was exhausted and depleted of calories which I wasn't supplying.

I found a campsite in a somewhat open area and there wasn't a level spot. Shortly before stopping, I had found some soft energy gels in a wrapper near the path. The hiker that I am, I picked them up and ate two. I was hoping I could hike several more miles but they only kept me from sleeping that night. The sky never reached the darkness I needed to sleep, but then I rolled to the entrance of the tent all night. My body never found sleep that night. I was scared, and that's something I didn't enjoy.

On July 19, I had 10 miles to go to reach the town of Twin Lakes. After eating ½ cup of cold mashed potatoes and a pack of tuna, I was ready to hike that morning. I wanted to call home and tell my mom what had happened. And that I had decided to stay on the trail. The side trail to the 2nd highest mountain in Colorado was just steps from where I had camped.

By 6:30 a.m., I had greeted some 30 day hikers who were all summiting Mount Massive at 14,421 feet that day. It was a Sunday morning, and everyone thought they were the first to tackle the 3,350 foot climb to the summit.

I was asked, "Did you already summit?"

My answer that morning was, "No, I'm hiking the Colorado Trail. I hike trails and climb mountains if they are part of the trail."

My two breakfast bars and the three gels that I had found the day before on the trail had to last me for 10 miles.

Dreaming of a hot shower and food, I was gliding down the trail. The three miles to the Mount Massive Trailhead were an enjoyable walk filled with short chats with day hikers who were heading up Mount Massive.

Colorado has 54 mountains which are above 14,000 feet, and 2/3 of those are within 20 miles of the Colorado Trail. When someone is speaking of a fourteener, they are referring to a mountain that is above 14,000 feet. Colorado is the only Rocky Mountain state which has all of its fourteeners within a 120-mile radius centered in the Sawatch Range near Buena Vista. Although Wyoming and New Mexico have the same geological history, they lack the fourteeners.

While taking a break and treating some water from the Halfmoon Creek, I was joined by a day hiker who was just discovering hiking. He introduced himself as Tom and I fell silent for a moment. Please God, stop sending men with the name Tom! He asked questions about long distance hiking and the best way to get into shape. Coming from a flat state,

he was stopping often to gain his breath. We parted ways at the Mount Elbert Trail. Mount Elbert is the highest mountain in Colorado. It towers at 14,433 feet.

As I continued hiking that day, I followed the well-marked trail which would lead me to Twin Lakes. The batteries in my camera had finally died, and I so wanted a few pictures of my day hiking into Twin Lakes; however, I will always have images etched in my memory. The first picture would have been of the aspens that lined the sides of the path with a snow-covered mountain in the distance. Wanting to hold on to the moment, I hiked ever so slowly down the trail and gazed at the leaves that were dancing and waving above me.

As I'm sitting here writing, an Instagram by Todd Chrisley comes to mind. "While you can't control someone's negative behavior you can control how long you participate in it." And that's a reminder to myself as well because I can be that negative person who needs to find that positive place within at times. Our own minds can keep us there for too long when we question other people's actions or lack thereof. They may never remember what they have said or done, and we hold on to it for way too long. Those thoughts need to be replaced with productive images that are helpful in our lives.

Before heading down the gravel road that led into Twin Lakes, I came across a large beaver dam that occupied the pond. This is the second image which is now stored in my mental folder of astounding impressions. After filling my eyes and mind with marvelous views, I was ready to fill my body with some much needed calories.

Coming up on the main road, I turned left and passed the first available diner. A hamburger van was located just off the road with patio furniture in the yard. I gave it a miss and headed for the Twin Lakes Inn. The rustic, green, tin-roofed, two-story inn had green wooden shutters with carved Christmas trees in the middle. I knocked at the door, and a

lean, fit gentleman with a rough, deep voice allowed me access. Checking the computer, he and the manager were able to find the one cancellation that I required. I arrived at 2 p.m. and took the afternoon to collect my thoughts, repackage my food, shower, wash clothes, and eat.

After paying for two nights, I dropped my backpack and crossed the small gravel road to the General Store. I checked the shelves, but my second orange five-gallon bucket wasn't to be found.

Then I happened to say, "My resupply was in a bucket."

And the younger lady said, "Why didn't you say that at first?! I put it in the back room because it was too out of place in the store."

The store and the other accommodations were open for only six months a year. The store was run by a young couple and his parents. It had a wide selection of hiking essentials and some extra items for the non-hiker. They would allow packages to be sent to their store free of charge. The shelves and closet held all sizes of boxes and two five-gallon buckets this summer. From the look of the boxes, there were a number of hikers behind me.

The younger gentleman informed me, "We work hard for six months and then ski." The younger lady, who had a little one, didn't seem as pleased with the arrangement, but it sounded nice if you're a winter person. I'm the opposite. I work during the winter and hike in the summer. We all desire something, and it's important to seek that.

mountains / hardships

July 20, 2015, turned out to be my second and final zero day on this adventure. Twin Lakes is an old mining town and possibly the oldest resort town as well. I took the opportunity to stretch my legs on a historical self-guided walking tour of this town. The Twin Lake Inn was built in 1882 and has had several names over the years. In addition to being a hotel and tavern, ladies of the evening had been known to entertain miners on the property. Each room was named after such a lady and the larger rooms were named after the mountains close by.

Bessie's Room is where I stayed and draped my wet clothes that were washed in the shower with me. The town isn't able to support a laundromat because everyone is on a well and septic system. The plaque on the wall outside the room stated, "This room is dedicated to Bessie (last name unknown), a 'Lady of the Evening,' who is believed to have worked this room from 1886 to 1892. Bessie was a hearty, salt-of-the-earth woman who could hold her own with people of every degree from the roughest to the most refined, and her friendly good humor made her well-liked by all."

My stay at the Inn became a highlight of this hike. I met new people, and I had a long talk with my mom about Tom. I'm sorry that it came to this, but I just couldn't allow him to think he can treat me or anyone the way he did. I was no longer going to participate in a relationship that was harming me physically and emotionally. I continue praying that he will find the help he requires, and the happiness I wasn't able to give him. While trying to be the wife he wanted, I was becoming another person.

Now I was walking around a small town in the middle of Colorado. A place in which past hardships were still visible. One of my favorite sites was Patrick Ryan's sod building which was built around 1880. It is about three feet below the earth's surface with six stacked logs above the surface. It even has several windows which were very expensive in those days. After all the years of wind and rain, the sod cabin is still standing, and I was able to see it and sympathize with the ladies who had to live in such conditions. The schoolhouse was being renovated and many other buildings are in excellent shape.

We go through difficult times and come out a better person on the other side. Renovating our thoughts and actions is

sometimes crucial to saving a relationship. If one feels there is no problem then nothing changes. Static. Each issue can fester into an immense matter and one becomes motionless and disconnected from the individual. That's why the Bible is so clear about not provoking, pestering, offending, displeasing, annoying, or enraging and the list of negative actions goes on. Life is a mountain and how we climb it is who we are.

After touring the town and eating another meal, I was ready for the day to end so I could finish this hike and head home to my grandchildren. The older two were having fun with their friends, but I wanted to spend time with Kayleigh and Braxton. He was born at the end of April and I was missing his first few months. On my return, his mother would start working again, and I would be able to watch them a few times a month. I so enjoy my time with my grandchildren! And now Kayleigh enjoys swimming and it's something we do together. Pixie hunting and swimming are our things.

I woke up several times, waiting for the birds to sing so I could pack up my belongings and head down for breakfast. Finally, I heard a car drive by and I was up. I had breakfast with an elderly gentleman named Bill and we spoke about the trail and his adventures out west. He was heading to Washington in a few days to hike Mount Rainier. He offered a ride to the trailhead and saved me an hour of non-trail hiking.

Starting early, I wasn't exposed to the hot sun. My walk along the shoreline of Twin Lakes was perfect. The sun was popping out of the slightly grey sky. The valley was covered in sagebrush and yellow flowers. I reached the East/West divide and I was feeling good about completing six miles already. How many could I hike today? The Colorado Collegiate West would take hikers over Mount Hope which was almost a fourteener, at 13,933 feet. The more traveled path is Collegiate East which is the path I would be traversing.

be free

As I entered the large forest of ponderosa pines, a loud thunderstorm was ready to dump some rain on me. I quickly found a full tree that would deflect some rain, and I sat under it. This is a no-no, but it worked for me on this experience. There were so many trees around. What are the chances that lightning would hit the one I was sitting under? That was my logic and my wilderness training. I covered my backpack and sat there eating a snack as another hiker called Chaps suited himself up in a rain jacket and pants. He walked on in the rain and I remained until it stopped.

For the next 13 miles, we would leapfrog each other through the dead forest. I took my rain jacket off and put it on again several times before I reached the ridge near Clear Creek Valley. Coming over the ridge, I was bewildered at the sight before me. There was life in the valley. Clear Creek snaked along the valley floor and there were large green fields. I sat there watching the dump trucks deliver gravel on the road below. Moments before, I had seen burnt trees and no life. But the valley which housed the Clear Creek Reservoir was teeming with life.

After a 30-minute break, I descended the ridge on switch-backs that reached the road below. Crossing the road and walking through the campground, I noticed several car campers and horse trailers. I was low on water, so I stopped before the bridge crossing and filled my bladder.

Before starting a five-mile climb, I took the opportunity to soak my feet in the cool river. Though I wanted to lay down in the grass, I decided to tackle the next mountain which would be almost a 3,000-foot climb. On the dusty foot-path, I placed one foot in front of the other. It was a slow climb, and I was depleted of energy that afternoon. The extra water weight added to my discomfort. Time to fuel the body. I found a spot where the sun was filtering through the branches, and that's where I sat for a spell.

After unpacking my cook set and food, I prepared a hot meal. My soup can and Esbit stove which I had purchased in Twin Lakes were working out well. Esbit cubes are small solid fuel items that heat up two cups of water. I had divided my two person meals into single servings, and I reused the resealable meal pouch to cut down on packaging. The other serving was packaged in a smaller zip lock bag. After leaving town, I try to eat the heavier items first. A thru-hiker should eat about two pounds of food a day, but I rarely carry that much food.

After consuming several hundred calories, I was ready to see how far my legs would carry me that late afternoon. The sky was blue and the temperature was perfect. In contrast, at this time of year the Appalachian Trail is a sweat box. A hiker develops a musty odor that is unique to the East Coast. And that smell permeates a hiker's backpack, clothes, and body. You can't escape the 100% humidity. Your clothes and body are never dry. And here I could hike mountains and never break a sweat.

It was time to start the steep ascent and enter Collegiate Peaks Wilderness Area. A Harvard Professor named Josiah Dwight Whitney surveyed the area peaks in 1869 starting with Mount Harvard at 14,420 feet. They started naming the fourteeners in this area after universities. And later climbers continued that practice. Shortly before sunset, I reached an outcrop that had a view of Mount Waverly at 13,292 feet. Within the next few miles, two other fourteeners - Mount Harvard at 14,420 feet and Mount Columbia at 14,073 feet - would be visible. All three mountains are within three miles of the Colorado Trail. Thinking that I was on the ridge, I decided to set up camp. It turned out to be an 18.6-mile day, and I slept above 10,000 feet.

On the morning of July 22, I took my time in camp. It had rained a bit throughout the night, and I wasn't in a hurry to pack up a wet tent. The sun hadn't reached my corner of the forest, and my fingers were cold. I was enjoying my warm, cozy bed in the tent. No rush. I was hiking the miles, and I figured August 10 would be my completion date.

Leaving camp, I was still climbing. I think I had stopped two miles short, making my previous day a 17-mile day. My journal entry states, "Seems like I only climbed today." Out of the 13.5 miles, about five were climbs. As I reached the first ridge, the area seemed planted and groomed. An English garden out of place at 11,845 feet.

I was passing hikers and hikers were passing me. Brightflower, who had hiked the Appalachian Trail in 2012, and her companion were just starting the day. I said, "Good morning," and then continued down the series of steep switchbacks. I met several old-timers who were out hiking part or all of the trail. Old School, who had everything from the '80s, was hiking with an umbrella but no hiking poles. And Glacier, who took every opportunity to stop and enjoy his surroundings, was hiking two sections this summer. Several friends were going to join him at the next stop.

This was the day I would see these forest dwellers often. I would stop, eat, and fill up my water, and they would pass me. When the sun was overhead, I stopped and dried out

everything. And it was the right time to lay back and soak in the rays. On the tundra, I viewed the snowcapped mountains in the distance and examined all the petrified wood that littered the surrounding area. There was so much to see and not enough hours in the day to see it all. I wanted to sit there and continue my soaking. But if I stayed any longer, I wouldn't descend to 10,000 feet before nightfall.

Evening was approaching and I had passed several suitable campsites. On the Appalachian Trail, it was nice coming into camp where others were, but here I found my time alone with God so rewarding. I spoke with Him throughout the day and He was always there listening. How did He give so much of Himself to me? On my Appalachian Trail thru-hike in 2011, I was angry with God. On many occasions, I cried and refused to speak with Him. And here He and I were communing all day long. I didn't want to share that time with anyone. Smiling and being at peace with myself and being in the presence of God was all that I required at that time. I felt complete.

dry

Waterfront property was my spot for the night. Harvard Lakes was my last stop before exiting Collegiate Peaks Wilderness Area, and this is where I pitched my tent. Before retiring, I watched the fish perform a fascinating show near the shore of Harvard Lakes. It was another enchanting place on this adventure. Unable to sleep, I rose and became a spectator of the late night show. So many stars were twinkling in the still lake. The forest was quiet and only the stars were performing.

The batteries in my headlamp gave out that evening, and I decided to pack up in the moonlight. It was a warmer night, and I thought a night hike was the thing to do. I had greeted an elderly couple the evening before as they came down a small hill, so I knew the trail went up. After I had crossed three logs and a creek, the moon disappeared and the forest became very dark. I stopped and pulled out my Tyvek to sit on and slipped my jacket and gloves on. Tyvek, the housewrap used during construction, is useful to hikers as a water barrier under tents, lightweight, and easy to pack. Finally, I wrapped my quilt around me and then waited for daylight. As I sat there, I could hear the water flowing which drowned out any other forest sounds. But I couldn't see anything. It was pitch black.

After some time, the forest started waking up. I had missed a large bog area by a few feet. Having hiked just over 200 miles and after consuming a full meal the night before, I was moving faster. Was my body in hiker shape? As I glided down the path, I observed the sky changing colors as the sun scaled the mountain across the valley. I stopped as the golden ball appeared once again to warm my body. Two day hikers came up the trail as I was taking a picture of a distant bare mountain. Could this be the unnamed 13,000-foot peak in the Collegiate Peaks Wilderness Area?

I reached North Cottonwood Creek just after sunrise, had breakfast, and filled up on water. After finding a path across the creek, I came upon Glacier who had stopped at that very spot and was sitting in a rocking chair which was in the forest. He had sat in it until 10 p.m. the night before. Glacier is so named because he moves very slowly. Another reason why agendas aren't a good idea. You just never know when you want to stop and enjoy the moment.

Kristian Eck, a Facebook pal, states it so well, "When your world moves too fast and you lose yourself in the chaos, introduce yourself to each color of the sunset (or sunrise.) Reacquaint yourself with the earth below your feet. Thank the air that surrounds you with every breath you take. Find yourself in the appreciation of life." Bubbling with excitement, I stood there gazing at the rocking chair that had become a symbol of pleasure for that hiker. We may not have all the facts to see the big picture in some situations, but we can appreciate the beauty before us. No matter how insignificant it may be to others.

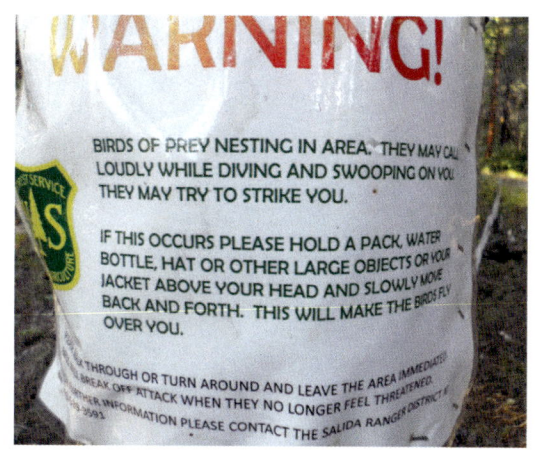

The sign before me was a warning sign. The facts were clear. Birds of prey were nesting in the area, and they might swoop down to attack hikers. In hopes that they would fly away, I was to wave something above my head to distract them. Only one hiker, Old School, passed me on this arduous climb. In less than four miles, I would ascend nearly 2,500 feet with no switchbacks.

Before re-entering the Collegiate Peaks Wilderness Area, I would have to clamber on this dry narrow path on the edge of the mountain. It was a vertical climb like none I had encountered on this trail so far. Old School used his umbrella as he hiked past me. And that's the last time I saw him. The sun beat down, and the dust spiraled up with each step. I encouraged myself with each break. It was only 3.4 miles to the summit. How hard could it be? I was moving like a snail, but I was going forward. I wasn't going to win any race that morning.

Once I reached the top, I sat under a tree in a small grove. I examined my data book and realized that I was on the first summit. Climbing a bit further, I was once again in another world. The remains of a small cabin were sheltered on this plateau. As I followed Silver Creek, I couldn't fathom how so much water could keep

flowing down the creek which was at the top of a mountain. The noise of the water was deafening.

I crossed Silver Creek for the last time and headed into the dense forest filled with natural moss sculptures. The stumps were lined with several species of moss. I could think only of Kayleigh, my youngest granddaughter, who enjoys pixie hunting with Nana. This was the forest where I would find the pixies. Creating stories in my head, I enjoyed my short stay in the fascinating world of fairyland creatures. Finally, I summited the saddle on the east ridge of Mount Yale at the 3.4-mile mark. I could produce the selfie which is proof of my feat of conquering this difficult climb. And I snapped it for that very reason. Not just anyone could scale this mountain.

A wonderful person back home says it so well, "Each day is another step on the path of your future. What you do today directs where you will be tomorrow. Don't spend today focused on yesterday, last week, last month, or last year.

Today, take a step closer to your dreams and the desires of your heart. Daily baby steps will take you farther than standing still." As life and the trail became drier, I moved forward with a positive attitude and a happier heart because I believed in myself and who I am as a person. I am a "Doer."

really dry

It's bewildering that you can sometimes so clearly remember events, and then there is part of a day that has been erased from your memory. That's how I feel about the next few miles and hours on the trail. My journal is empty and the dictation slim. I was entering horse country and the trails were sandy. Several creek beds were dry. No more snow-capped mountains in the distance; however, I spotted a new deep purple flower. The picture doesn't do it justice.

On July 23, I started night hiking in the early hours, watched as the sun made its entrance on the new day, saw an unusual piece of furniture in the middle of the forest, encountered a warning sign, ambled up a monstrous peak, passed a homestead or hunting cabin, visited with the pixies for a spell, and descended into dry horse country; this all happened within a 16.3-mile stretch of this captivating trail. I drank my fill of the spectacular views before me each and every day.

Trekking through a bent aspen forest, I was eager to find water. Instead, I entered a parking lot and searched for the next CT marker that would steer me in the right direction. As I made an about-face turn, two young ladies were unloading their backpacks from a cab. Passing up the bathroom, I crossed the parking lot and headed down a small bank before turning left on the trail. Too much civilization in a short span and I was confused. Confronted with people, parking lots, and a road which led to Buena Vista, I became disoriented. I questioned the data book and my skills in navigating. Once I was back on track, I was anxious to leave society behind. But the next several days were filled with people. Bikers, hikers, runners, and horseback riders descended on the trails in the Hot Springs area.

The two young ladies who exited the cab were on a 40-mile hike to check out their stuff, a shake-down hike. They want to hike the Pacific Crest Trail, PCT, which runs from Mexico to Canada, a more than 2,600-mile trek, in 2016. It would take them through California, Oregon, and Washington. One had hiked several miles on the PCT already, and her gear was tested; however, the other was still packing heavy items. The first thing I noticed was the large cup which was dangling from her pack. She also had some difficulty climbing the steady incline which we encountered leaving the parking lot. We passed each other several times as we ascended the two-mile, less than 1,000-foot climb. The afternoon was warm and the lack of water made it a rather tiresome slog. I told myself, "I'm going to stop at the first water source."

Once I reached 10,000 feet, I was ready to stop at any time. A small creek was flowing and now I needed to find a level piece of real estate. I ambled up the other side of the creek for about 50 feet and found a spot that still had sun. After setting up my tent, I went back to the under-sized creek and commenced with my evening duties. I treated several liters of water and washed my body and clothes in the shallow creek bed. The sun was still shining, so the clothes would dry before night fall.

Devouring my last meal, I was thrilled about arriving in Hot Springs the following day. On the Appalachian Trail, I arrived in Hot Springs, North Carolina, after a "nero," hiking only a few miles (near zero) in a day. Because my gear was wet then, I dried everything out and bought a synthetic sleeping bag. I shipped my down bag home. As time went on, I changed other gear items on that hike, but here I had changed only my cooking method because Tom had the stove. I had passed up the springs then, but I wanted to partake in them this time.

On the ridge, I felt the evening warmth as the sun set across the next mountain. Having had several clear, warm, cloudless days, I was delighted with my decision to continue the hike. I had realized that I need to be responsible for my well-being and future happiness. I am accountable for my reactions to situations and how I deal with other people's behavior. How long I participate in other people's negative or disrespectful behavior is up to me. Sometimes the best thing to do is to walk away. One thing I do well is walk!

The following morning, I had a dry, warm hike into Hot Springs. Once I passed a large wooden sign stating:

> Colorado Trail 1776
> Traveling Through Private
> Property for .7 miles
> Please Stay On Trail.

All of this was in capital letters. I was on dirt roads and then finally on a paved road that led into Hot Springs. But first, I trudged down a staircase that led into a Christian youth camp, Frontier Ranch. Somehow, I had missed a sign. I had a great ride in a golf cart through the camp to the service entrance. It was an awesome sight to behold. In this dry land, youth were experiencing the Wild West through several different activities. A group of girls had come to the office and Bev explained what I was doing. They had hiked several miles the day before and couldn't fathom hiking 486 miles, let alone 2,181 miles!

Once I was on the right course, I hiked into Hot Springs. Crossing the road, I entered the small grocery store and checked on a few items. A nice-sized beef burrito and a pint of strawberry ice cream were my lunch. I contemplated the springs and the restaurant, but I gave them both a miss. In 22 miles, I would be picking up a large resupply and stop to shower. Corona Sam and Grizzle had buried a bucket just outside of Hot Springs. Hoping I would stumble on the loot, I bought only a few things.

After downing my lunch, I chatted with Eric on the hotel phone for a few minutes. And then I headed out of town on the paved road. The Chalk Cliffs were visible in the distance. The granite has been altered to white clay by the spring water running over them.

Stopping several times to drink and check my data book, I was pleased to reach a shady road that maneuvered through a humble neighborhood. There were several quaint, charming, mountain chalets. The well-groomed yards and flowers were being watered.

Once I reached the trail head for section 14, I was ready for another treasure hunt. Corona Sam and Grizzly had buried another bucket just up from the parking area. I read my note a second time, and then I followed the clues. Crossing the well-constructed bridge, I started scouting for a large log on the right. It was easy to spot and I clambered over the log. Under the pile of branches, I uncovered an extra resupply. The tuna packs and extra power bars would be added weight. But the supplements were greatly needed as I continued the roller coaster daily trek.

Chalk Creek was the last reliable water source for the next 6.6 miles. It was a dry, hot day. I ate a few things from the bucket, and then I sealed and re-buried the bucket. It was time to climb the 1.5-mile ascent. As I flung myself onto this mountain, I met a family with a young boy. I asked the parents if they would like to go on treasure hunt. I gave them the one small sheet of notebook paper so they could go hunting for the bucket I had reburied a few minutes earlier. "Leave no trace." They were removing the bucket for me.

I had bought two Power drinks in Hot Springs, and I finished the second one as I was hiking uphill. At the top of the climb, there were sticks laid out on one side of the trail. I guess it was a deterrent so that hikers and other trail users would stay on the marked trail. To me, it was wilderness art sculpted by man. As I sat under a small, twisted pine tree, I consumed more water. This was the hottest day on the trail. It may have been in the low 80s. I had drunk 4 liters already, and I had another five miles to go through this desert-like environment.

Contentment is what I desire in my life. I had found gratification in this day, and I was content with my situation. If something isn't working, I choose to change the present circumstances that I face. In life, we have the choice to arrange things that fit us. You can have a dry, meaningless future or you can do something about your situation. Find what makes you happy.

treasures

Upon summiting this minor knoll at 9,310 feet, I experienced the meaning of heaven and earth as I ambled through the next few miles. The pine trees were spaced apart in small groups. One lonely bush was calling me to take its picture. Like the burning bush that Moses faced in the Bible, it was an attention getter. What was I to learn on this stretch of the hike?

On earth, we tend to associate ourselves with like-minded individuals and those that we can tolerate being around. And here I was seeing the trees as people. It's not something God wants from us, but it's difficult to be around unlovable people. I could very well be that kind of person. So, how can I change? To be a lovable person, one must develop traits such as love, joy, peace, long-suffering, kindness, goodness, faithfulness, gentleness, and self-control. The Bible calls these the Fruit of the Spirit. A wonderful package, but what is the key to having all of them as part of your life?

I felt the peace, and the rain was all around me. My small world, at that moment, wasn't touched by the precipitation that streamed perfectly from the sky. A ragamuffin of a man passed me during my revelation. He was the most unlikely hiker. His backpack was an external framed canvas with gear strapped to the outside, and his clothes were on the heavy side. Ones that would take days to dry if they got wet. This slender, out-of-place man was just what I needed to see.

On the Appalachian Trail, when I reached Great Barrington, Mass., a section hiker remembered me from GA. His first comment was, "I can't believe you're here!" We stereotype and judge people without cause. Walking forward, I noticed that the trees were different heights and shapes. Yet they stood tall in this forest that seemed groomed. People who hike come in all shapes and heights, but their character develops overtime. They too need grooming in order to stand tall through life's trials.

During Thanksgiving 2015, I hiked the horse trail from Elk Garden, VA. The sky was blue with a few passing clouds and the temperature was in the low 50s. A big difference from the blizzard conditions I had experienced during the first week of November in 2010! It was perfect hiking weather. After a three-week battle with bronchitis, this felt like a walk in the park. I'm thankful that I'm well enough to hike the miles once again.

There are so many things I'm thankful for. Being so close to my three adult sons is something I treasure daily. Having a friend in Julie, who is there to listen even though she is as far left on political issues as it comes. After a meltdown a few weeks ago, she listened and then texted, "I love you." It was a shock to see, but I felt so valued. Religion and politics aside, she has shown me unconditional love. A friend who's there during the good and bad times.

My son Eric had a conversation with a family member the other day and he shared it with me. Apparently, this family member said, "You know how your mom is." And Eric replied, "No, I don't know what you mean. My mom's great and some people could learn something from her." How proud and honored I was to hear something of this nature. This is the greatest compliment a mother could receive. There are many things I count as treasures, but this could count as a treasure laid up in heaven. This refers to doing good and how it will reflect in heaven. He has also stated, "Mom, I can't worry about what others say or do. What happened in the past is in the past." God heals, and Eric is moving forward with his healing process.

In the future, I hope to hear, "Well done, good and faithful servant." That will be my ultimate treasure.

trail journal entries

July 24, 2015   *16.6 miles plus extra miles*

The day was filled with excitement and revelation. As the afternoon progressed, I was counting my blessings and reflecting on my treasures. Is it stuff that I covet or relationships? I have always wanted to share my sons with others because they have so much love and goodness to share. But you can't make people want to be around. Jealousy can destroy a relationship in a heartbeat. With jealousy comes manipulation and then the trust and love fades. Trust issues can hinder a relationship. When you add fear into the mix, you have a big mess.

A lot of these issues came to a head on that afternoon just one week before. I'm not willingly going to allow someone to manipulate me or situations. And I'm not in the market for jealousy. They aren't becoming character traits. Facebook today said I was, "Encouraging, calm, and tasteful." I think the tasteful part comes into play with how I speak with others because I'm not a fashion person; unless my hiking clothes count!

Leaving my dreamland, I was facing reality once again. I was losing daylight and ready for a campsite. As I approached Browns Creek, I could hear people playing in the water. I picked up my pace and examined the next sign only to take the wrong turn. I questioned the long ridge walk, but put it down to being tired. And then I was at the Browns Creek Trailhead. Man, I wasn't going to stop until I reached a Colorado Trail sign. I scrambled up a water drainage system. On I went for a mile and a half, and I had once again summited the Browns Creek Waterfall area. Finding a flat area, I set up my tent as daylight faded rapidly. Almost a 20-mile day but only 16.6 miles on the CT. I had only 17 ounces of water left. The data book showed water in 2 ½ miles but that would be a task for the next day. I needed sleep.

July 25, 2015   14 miles

I slept so well that I had a later start. The sun was hitting the tent, and I knew that it was time to start my day. This was the people day. I stopped and chatted with everyone. Horse riders, bikers, hikers, and young and older couples. Some people were resting and others were having a picnic under a tree. Everyone was out enjoying the nice warm day. I came upon the first couple shortly after packing up. The first question out of my mouth was, "How far to the next water supply?"

"Just around the bend," the young man said.

On my first break of the day, I ate a moon pie and drank a liter of water. After treating two more liters, I was ready for some miles. A mounted trail maintenance crew came from behind. While chatting with two ladies at the end, I asked about riding on these narrow paths.

One piped up, "Horses have four legs. They can balance on three easy enough."

They also shared how the section near Browns Creek wasn't marked very well. Seems as though they had ridden several extra miles the day before. After hand sawing a few smaller trees that were across the path, they vanished out of sight as fast as they had arrived. Upon reaching the top, I was ready for another break.

This time I sat under a tree, and watched the next riders on horseback coming through the trees. A relaxed bunch of people who were pleased that something was carrying them up the mountain. They weren't out of breath, nor were they exerting any energy. I did think about riding the next few miles, but that sure would cost a lot of money. And I had two strong legs that were doing the job.

The other memorable conversation was with the older couple who were picnicking in the shade.

"Hi there," is all I heard.

I looked in all directions and couldn't find the individual who said that. Again I heard, "Hi, you hiking the Colorado Trail?" And then I saw the couple.

"Yes, I am," I replied.

We spoke for a few more minutes, and then the gentleman said, "You'll find the pixies dancing down the trail under the large pine." I was on my way to finding the dancing pixies.

The last few miles into Salida were uneventful. I was looking forward to a shower and possible rest day. But first I needed to hitch a ride to the two campgrounds and track down my resupply. A biker was resting near a dump truck. He was the biker I had met in Hot Springs. His legs had given out, and his wife was picking him up.

A few cars passed me, and then one turned around. J and Kat, who is from Germany, were my saving grace that afternoon. I told them of my situation, and they were eager to help. The first campground knew nothing of my resupply. So, we drove to the next one a few miles further. As I asked the two attendants, they had a look of bewilderment about them. Although they were so close to the trail, they had no idea what I was talking about. Explains why it's so difficult to resupply on this trail. Just as I was explaining, a woman stepped into the office.

She said, "Her stuff is in that black plastic bag." Relief! This was my last convenient resupply for some 100 miles. I had food, and now had to repackage it. I decided to have a lift back to the trail and pass up a shower. Sitting on the side of the trail, I finished selecting my food and gave the rest to three young guys who were car camping.

Not wanting to camp near the road, I started the nine-mile climb. After two miles, I realized I would be among people that night. I needed to decide on a camping spot. I stopped near the creek, so I could wash myself and my hiking clothes.

July 26, 2015   *14.2 miles*

What a peaceful hike through the forest! I had a cold night, and the first few miles were cool. As I passed several more campers that morning, I began hiking the steady seven-mile ascent which would peak at 11,908 feet. It was such an enchanting hike! The hikers who traversed the Collegiate West joined the trail south again. The young woman who couldn't decide which route to take in Twin Lakes happened upon me that morning. She was heading back to Salida. She wanted to hike the Collegiate East as well.

As I slowly ambled through the forest, I had the company of two dogs. They were from the camping area, and they followed me for some time. I was carrying seven days' worth of food and two liters of water. Before summiting this mountain, I had six more miles of stair stepping. At the 8.2-mile mark, I refueled my body. The last mile was brutal because it was shale underfoot. Very loose rock that made me slide backwards as I tried to move forward up the mountain. I could hear other hikers cheering me on as I climbed. Whobbie, whom I met earlier, was waiting at the top. He snapped my favorite picture of me near the Fooses Creek Trail sign.

As we were taking each other's pictures, a local biker raced down the mountain we had just climbed. In two seconds, he had reached the bottom of that beast of a climb. Other bikers opted for another route off the top.

What a spectacular view! The clouds were there, but the sun was out. Bikers and dirt bikes passed me on this section. As I heard the dirt bikes in the distance, I would step off the trail for them to pass. It must have been a weekend because there were people everywhere. Ones who were there and then gone. And then the slower hikers who took every opportunity to experience and view the surroundings. I began rationing my food because I wasn't certain if there would be any in 40 miles. While taking a break at the top, I spun around several times trying to remember this fabulous view.

Reaching the next ridge, I ended the day with 14 plus miles and no rain. I found a camp area with a log for seating and a fire pit. The most important part was the flat ground. After setting up camp, I placed myself in the last bit of sunlight.

July 27, 2015   *15.5 miles*

How well I slept in my tent! I told myself, "This is nice." I had the perfect campsite, and that morning, I had a visitor. The largest hare, still wearing a thick winter coat, came bouncing up to my tent. Mesmerized by his presence, I stood there watching him for what seemed like an eternity. I was part of Alice in Wonderland! Waiting for him to speak, I continued watching his movements. When he finally headed into the woods, I completed my morning chores and proceeded with my job, hiking. A beautiful sunrise over the mountaintop and a visit from Mr. Hare were an awesome start to the day.

As I maneuvered through the boggy parts that had been created by the motorcyclists, I met several other hikers. The "Four Wonder Ladies" were out hiking the trail together and Hurricane, a man from New Zealand, was hiking the Continental Divide National Scenic Trail, known as the Continental Divide Trail, which winds from Mexico to Canada through five western states. About 234 miles of the Colorado Trail is part of the Continental Divide Trail as well.

At one point, I sat under a tree with my rain gear on. While I was waiting for the rain to move on, a motorcyclist passed. Then I hiked through cow country for several miles. Wall Street had joined me near a muddy cow spot which had the first reliable water. Finding a place where the water was

flowing was challenging, but in the end I managed to fill up my two-liter bladder. We chatted for a spell, and then I continued my trek through cow country. It turned out to be the million dollar view of the day. The cows were my late afternoon companions as I had my snack.

At 15 miles, my feet and the rest of my body wanted to give up, but my mind wanted to go on. I just couldn't do any more. Checking on my calories for the day, I realized I had eaten only around 1,700 calories, and I was burning 4,000

plus. At that rate, I was losing a pound every two days. I hoped that I would come across a resupply at the end of the next day's hike, so I could have a feast.

As I finished my break, Chris, a photographer, was positioning himself to capture the first cyclists who were riding from Durango to Denver. One cyclist wanted to complete this adventure in 3 ½ days. My cow country day ended at the Sargents Mesa sign. Several cows approached me with caution and entertained me for some time that splendid afternoon. I hiked for another 2.4 miles, and set up my tent off trail as the day was coming to an end.

July 28, 2015   20.5 miles

The remainder of section 17 was filled with PUDs, "pointless up and downs," which defined my hiking for the day. In seven days, I had pushed my body and completed 107 miles. Biker Steve, whom I met in Hot Springs and again in Salida, was back on the trail. He had taken several days off to rest his legs, and now he wanted to see an end to this task.

Biker Steve stated, "You're the fastest south-bounder hiking the trail from Denver to Durango out here." We chatted for a bit about Scott, who had just set the fastest supported hike on the Appalachian Trail. And the conversation ended with the cyclists who were now on the CT.

Shortly after our chat, a cyclist from Asheville, NC, was pushing his bike up the hill. He was contemplating quitting because the altitude was affecting him. I tried to encourage him, and I hope he was able to finish.

As the day went on, I came upon Steve again. "I've never passed a biker before!" I blurted out.

And then I passed him a second time. Steve said, "Go for it." On the downhill sections, he would fly by me. As he passed, he shouted, "See you in a bit!" I replied, "You're gone now!"

On the third pass, Steve jokingly said, "Go ahead, speed demon."

As I continued on another PUD, I bellowed, "This has to be the last climb in this section!"

Biker Steve echoed up the hill, "400 feet to the top."

I screeched, "There is a top!" And there I sat, ate something, and waited for Biker Steve for the last time.

I didn't know if that was on the 27th or 28th. I may have lost a day somewhere, and my recorder was full. Pen and paper were used for the rest of my hike. It was a great day for pushing myself and having another person to share in it was priceless. Going forward at a good speed, I felt like I had reached my total hiker shape.

On the 28th, I reached Lujan Creek where four young girls were camping for the night. The orange bucket there was filled with trash and no resupply was found. After eating a hot meal and soaking my feet, I found extra energy to attack the next climb in section 18.

July 29, 2015   26.2 miles

Waking up before daybreak proved to be very beneficial on this section of the trail. The day started out warmer, and it continued to be the warmest day on the trail. The change in the terrain and scenery had me contemplating how difficult the desert hike would be on the Pacific Crest Trail. The guidebook stated that a reliable water source was nonexistent on this stretch. I needed to prepare myself for a 21-mile hike to the next water supply.

Traveling on dirt ranch roads, I had the feeling I was hiking through Death Valley. The few flowers I saw were drooping and the dust was flying around as I shuffled my feet across the desert-like terrain. A lonely shrub was my shade for my first break. I was thankful that I had started the day early. But the long range views of the valley were something out of a Wild West movie. A lone hiker crossing the open prairie could be a character in the next tale.

Coming upon a seasonal spring, I climbed down the man-made run-off to consume another liter of water. I drank four liters while crossing this section. And I was expelling the liquid as fast as I was drinking it. On a small stretch, trees seemed to have been planted. As on the Camino Santiago in Spain, they provided hikers with some shade. Seeing the next tree-lined area, I was so excited that I had hiked some 14 miles before lunch. I was proud and I gave myself a lot of praise that day. It was a difficult task crossing that dry valley.

As I was praising myself, I recalled a time when my eldest son, who was then seven, said, "Mom, you're praising me too much." That was a memorable parenting moment! I rethought my parenting techniques and realized that my children also needed to experience some real life situations. I couldn't shelter them from all the hurts of the world. They needed to be exposed to all kinds of circumstances so that they could learn how to handle life. I continue to learn and relearn things each and every day.

As I headed down the valley near Cochetopa Creek, I came to a perfect spot. I slid down into the creek for a good wash after that dusty walk. After washing my hair and clothes, I felt much cleaner. Draping my wet clothes over several bushes, I started planning on hiking a 26.2-mile day. This would be the only section in which I could possibly accomplish such a mission. I would need to hike only 5.2 more miles. Could I do it?

I had a snack, put on my damp clothes, and I was on my way. A young couple with a barking dog were camping a few feet from me and that was another reason why I continued hiking that afternoon. Seems as though everyone was stopping at the first water source. A speedy couple who had plowed past me several miles earlier were settled in their tent already. They peeped out as I shuffled past them. They had said barely two words earlier and said nothing now. And that was fine, because I finally comprehended that my purpose on this trip was to be with my best friend and comforter,

God. I was exhilarated with each waking moment I had with Him. On the Appalachian Trail, I was angry and upset with God. And here, I wanted only Him.

Reaching a boggy area, I searched for the bridge so I could cross the rapidly flowing creek. Pushing through the bog and low shrubs, I fumbled and slipped into the brackish water. Backtracking, I gazed across the creek and located a wooden circular marker. I needed to cross the creek and climb a rock formation, and then I would be on the trail once again. Once I reached the top of the boulder, I had a hot meal.

An evening hiker passed me as I picked up my pace on this rather easy stretch. He agreed that stopping early in the day made for a long evening. It was much nicer to sample the woods at all times of the day. Even night hiking is filled with so many favorable events, such as staring at the bright moon or stars that shine in the heavenly realms. Not only can you behold the wonders of the night, but the night sounds are overwhelming.

As sunset was rapidly approaching, I increased my pace. I watched the fading sun's shadow inch its way up the mountain. Daylight was slipping away and I felt the cooler air on my hands. Drawing near the Eddiesville Trailhead, I attained my goal for the day! Passing a ranchers' entrance, I managed to pinpoint an area just across from the fencing that separated me from the longhorn cattle. I set up the tent behind a large evergreen during the last few minutes of daylight.

I had pushed my body through a 26.2-mile day. It was time to sleep and recharge my body. In my slumber, I recalled the day's events and all at once, I was wakened by a loud shout, "Yee ha!" The sounds of a galloping horse and bells were just inches from my tent. Had I been dreaming? Was this really happening? Laying ever so still, I listened for any other clatter that would surround me that night. The coyotes howled in the distance. Were they reacting to the man-made commotion or communicating with one another? I dozed off for a bit, but I never had a deep sleep that night. I was restless.

July 30, 2015   *14.2 miles*

Just yesterday I was warm, and this morning there was frost on my tent. Packing up my gear, I was on a mission. Finding those mystery hoof prints was first on my list. Once on the trail, I checked the rocky path for any sign of horses. A sign displayed a recommendation that horses should not be ridden on this stretch. It was an exquisite section which followed the Cochetopa Creek for several miles. The grass in the valley was knee-high and there were ponds everywhere. I would call this the "Valley of 100 Lakes."

As I continued hiking that morning, I came upon the only bird species in Colorado which lives the entire year above the tree line. This tundra dweller is the ptarmigan. Ptarmigan are weak fliers which gave me the opportunity to capture this one on film as it crossed my path only a few feet away. This hardy alpine ground grouse was moving slowly through the knee-high grass that was saturated with white

blossoms. I wondered if it was injured because I had never experienced a bird moving so slowly. And then it migrated into the denser brush.

Shortly thereafter, a north-bounder passed me saying, "Moose have been sighted up ahead!"

Sluggishly, I clambered up the seven-mile trail. It was a 2,300-foot climb, and I was running out of food. This lush valley proved to be the home of a small, brown, black-faced, furry creature that liked an audience. My count of these animals climbed quickly in the succeeding days. The marmot encounters were amusing.

At the summit, I was discombobulated. Which way was the trail going? It wasn't very obvious to me. Checked my minimalist data book, I forged out on the path that seemed to be the right one. I was very thankful that it was a sunny, dry day because navigating the rocks which moved under your feet was challenging. After losing my balance on numerous occasions, I was relieved to set foot on a non-moving surface at the bottom. Seeing another climb ahead, my body gave out.

I set up the tent on the side of the trail, crawled in, and took a nap. After my shuteye, I cooked up a hot meal. Having

gained some energy, I decided to hike a bit more. Two hikers had just joined the trail from a jeep access point. They were heading for the Continental Divide Trail. Section 20 in the guidebook was an exhilarating hike through the La Garita Wilderness. For miles, I was the only hiker on the mountain.

Once I reached the top of the next climb, I sat by a pole and examined the data book. I also gaped at the magnificent view that was spread before me. I had just climbed the first peak in section 21, the San Luis Pass to Spring Creek Pass. I was doing this all alone. I'm a badass. My son Eric had texted me on the Appalachian Trail saying, "Mom, you're a badass!" Wow, I was genuinely hiking in the middle of the wilderness with nothing around me! The Colorado Trail guidebook states, "This is one of the most remote segments of The Colorado Trail and Snow Mesa can feel completely cut off from civilization."

After ascending my third peak of the day, numbered as 13111, I would have only 12.4 miles to food the next day. I hoped I would find the food because I would be out by then. My job now was to find a campsite, and there before me were a few trees and a wonderful flat spot. Several large logs were turned up to make a table and a couple of chairs.

It would be a nice homestead for the night. Since I had already eaten dinner, I just sat and admired my surroundings. Behind me was a rocky peak, and this became my fixation throughout the night.

Awaking several times, I was gifted with a different scene each time. As the full moon crept up the sky, it illuminated my campsite. There was no need for a headlamp that night. The moon looked as if it was sitting on top of the peak. Standing there during a bathroom break, I was mesmerized at the beauty, and how I was the only person for miles around. I saw none of the other hikers who camped near Cochetopa Creek. I was in my own bubble, and I was content to move forward in that fashion. How I wanted to capture every moment on film, but there's so much more to that enchanting night. Being in the wilderness with only my wits continued to amaze even me.

July 31, 2015   *13.9 miles*

Since I had stayed awake enjoying the night sky's late show, I slept in. My evening was filled with memories of a perfect night. It was a dry clear night with the most supreme golden ball suspended in the night sky. That image is forever etched in my brain. Words can't possibly describe how magnificent the view was. I had hiked 170 miles in ten days. My body needed the sleep. Next, it needed food.

Starting my day at 7 a.m., I was hiking toward a resupply. Being above the tree line on the majority of this section, I was very vigilant watching the weather patterns. I had enjoyed a few days of remarkable conditions, but I prepared myself for some changes in the near future. The wildflowers were a carpet of astonishingly vivid colors against the harsh surroundings.

Peaks were covered in rock and the tundra was laden with boulders of all sizes.

As I passed through rolling mountains and sub-alpine meadows, the grasses were filled with an assortment of wildflowers. I so wanted to linger in the open and inspect each crevice for another hidden jewel, but I knew I would run out of food soon. As I filled up my water bottle at a seasonal spring, I retrieved my last bit of food - a 2.5-ounce tuna pack and a pack of crackers. Following the narrow path through the tundra, I saw jagged rock formations and bushy alpine plants. And then the alpine sunflower came into view with its massive head turned toward the rising sun. With mountains behind me, I crossed and climbed several more peaks before traversing Snow Mesa.

Thunder clouds loitered overhead as I moved swiftly across the Mesa. This tabletop is above 12,000 feet and there was no form of shelter. A few small drainage areas were possible escape avenues from a lightning storm. I continued to pray as I almost ran across this enormous terrain. My feet were moving ever so fast. Each time I passed a drainage area, I wondered if it was time to seek shelter. As I reached the tree line, the hail started. I had another 1.4 miles descending 2,000 feet before I could begin my search for food.

Relieved that I had reached the parking lot at Spring Creek Pass, I read my note once more. It said, "From toilet walk toward Hwy 140 (it's 149) B/T road and parking down slope abt 20 ft. we placed the food. Green tape marks trees where buried. We will place more tape very easy to find." I went straight to where the X marked the treasure. It was time

for a feast. As I cooked a hot two-portion meal, I spoke with a couple on a motorcycle. They had weathered out the hail in the parking lot bathroom. It had been the cleanest one on the trail. It must have been checked and cleaned daily.

I scored, and I ate well that afternoon. My next decision - town or not? I had the loot and the repacking was done. So I went hiking. Giving up even the simple things: showers, clean clothes, and a bed; this hike was about being with God and myself. Human companionship wasn't an issue for me. I was so content with this arrangement.

Within a few minutes of leaving the parking lot, I could have drunk a "trail magic" beer or two which were placed on the trail by a Trail Angel with a note signed "South Dakota," but I walked on. I met Eats and Kido who are hiking the CDT. Eats said, "I need more protein in my diet." He was feeling weak. I told him that I had just deposited several items in an orange five-gallon bucket. We chatted for a few minutes, and then I was off. With a heavy resupply, I was feeling the weight. And the next section was a roller coaster. The highest point on the Colorado Trail would be attained the next day.

In life, we face hurdles which can overcome us physically and emotionally. But how we react during those times shows our character. Just the other day, I was faced with a situation where I agonized over my future actions concerning this ordeal. How should I handle the circumstances and be true to who I am? After I pursued my course, my son Shaun called and said, "I love you, Mom. I just want to tell you - you're a good person." Just like when in the wilderness, we face situations that need our instant attention, and we may torture ourselves over which path to proceed on. And then things work out because we made a decision to do something.

At that point, I was hiking up a dirt road; not where I wanted to stop. I wanted to find something off the road. Finally, I turned off the dirt road and headed into a small wooded area. It looked promising. I found several live trees and a flat area between them. Erecting the tent, I was eager to enter my domicile for the night. It was a 13.9-mile day. I stopped a bit short, but I'm glad because it started raining. I was dry, warm, and had **lots** of food. All was good.

August 1, 2015   *17.4 miles*

On this section, I would encounter a steady incline with several dips before reaching the highest point at 13,271 feet. Once I started hiking, I noticed that I was only 20 feet from the modest creek that flowed across the path. The trail was faint and nonexistent at times. My scouting skills came into good use here. As I maneuvered my way through, my guide wasn't a worn path but the rock cairns and wooden poles that had been erected. My nasty-tasting 20-gram power bar and the chocolate smoothie which I had enjoyed were no longer fueling my body. The rugged, rocky terrain and the cooler morning had robbed me of my calories.

At one point, I was ankle deep in a marshy area which was impassable except by going through the middle. And then I was on several short switchbacks through a forest. The forest floor was covered with yellow blossoms.

Large sunflowers also found refuge here. It felt bizarre to be hiking through a vast openness one minute and then to be searching for a path through the marsh which led into this peaceful forest full of life. All this within a few miles.

Once in the open again, I needed to move because my body was feeling the dampness. And all at once, I was viewing the Red Mountain. As dark rainclouds moved all around, this bright red mountain was shining in the distance. My views were spectacular! Words and pictures aren't able to express the majestic landscape that was before me. The rain finally moved in, and I negotiated steeper switchbacks on slippery rocks. And still, all of this was the most stunning vista I had ever laid eyes on. Not standing around long to eat, I started on the never-ending switchbacks.

As I passed sizable rock formations, the marmots darted in and out of their rocky homes. Their chirps sound like a fire alarm with dying batteries. A certain one enjoyed my company and he posed for me. Continuing my climb, I stopped often to examine the panorama of the valley below. Inching as close to the edge as I could, I was in awe of what I beheld. I was a fortunate soul to experience such an adventure.

The trail had some icy patches which made this climb difficult. And then I heard a rumble. It was moving closer, and I was exposed. The alpine brush became my place of refuge. Under the bushes, I lay flat for 20 minutes with my plastic garbage bag covering me. After that, I reached a summit on a rocky mountain, and I wrote in my notebook,"13,271." After taking a selfie, I moved on because the cold rain was coming down.

Once off this slippery mountain, I was hiking on easier terrain, and then I spotted a wooden pole with a large sign, "Highest Point - 13,271 FT - The Colorado Trail."

The last mountain was my false summit, but it so seemed like the highest point. With a quick selfie video and a picture, I plowed on.

I was running out of drinking water, but the clouds were still dumping liquid. Heading down the steep jeep trails, I was sliding on the mud. As I reached the bottom, a biker asked, "How far to a road?" My reply, "A tough go across rugged mountaintops." He wasn't going to make the trek. Two wet days had taken a toll on this man. I passed through the Carson Saddle historical mining area. Gold mining started in the 1860s, but silver became the precious metal of choice in the 1870s. The mining boom seemed to come in ten-year cycles. By the 19th Century, the richest mineral deposits were found near Red Mountain. And now the mining camps are silent and only the remains are scattered across this region.

It was a necessity for me to continue that cold afternoon. I would be out of water in a very short time. Leaving the wide, muddy, 4-wheeler trail, I stepped onto a narrow path that followed a valley.

My next encounter with a marmot was from a distance. He was sitting on top of a wooden Colorado Trail marker. His home was on the other side of this narrow path. As I approached, he jumped from his perch and stood his ground by the post.

It was time to decide on a campsite. Passing a weathered rock formation which reminded me of a castle, I could only think of this as a natural stronghold. A mansion for all the creatures who call this territory their home. Crossing a small stream, I knew this would be home for the night. I could see my breath, and I discerned that this would be the night when I would use my survival blanket.

I was in the wilderness with the wild animals all around me that night. The chirping by the marmots was drowned out by the coyotes on the mountain just across from my campsite. It rained throughout the night, but the full moon was another amazing one.

August 2, 2015   11.8 miles

In the morning, the clouds were floating over the valley, and night activity had ceased. The glen was silent. Rain, rain, rain... I hiked the entire day in the rain with only moments of relief. *(The remainder of this day is recounted in the Chapter,* Rerun *on page 1.)*

August 3, 2015   *12.4 miles*

Hail, sun, rain, and trail magic; it was a great day! It rained all night, and I was in no hurry to pack up. Hoping to dry out everything in the morning sun, I was complacent. Moving slower than normal, I examined the tent. It had withstood the monsoon. And I decided to keep hiking. There was no need to come off the trail.

It was a busy day for hikers, horse riders, and pack llama groups. There were people everywhere. The Stony Pass Road Trailhead is a great access point for day hikers. This historical road was constructed in 1879. It was used to transport supplies in and out for the mining community. It was short-lived and it became known as a "pretty rough ride."

I sat with the llama group for a spell because I had found a walkie-talkie on the trail, and I spoke on it to see whose it was. Catching up with them, I returned it; however, it belonged to another group. Just moments before, I had said to

myself, "I would so like a PB&J!" And what was I offered? A PB&J was my snack along with a homemade fruit bar. That was my moment without rain.

One minute, I was sitting in the sun and then the rain started again. I tried holding a conversation with the owner of the llama tour group, but the rain just pelted down. Getting cold, I picked up my pace. At the junction where the Colorado Trail diverges from the Continental Divide Trail, I waved and was out of sight. Hail was stinging my bare legs. I moved fast across this open terrain. The relatively flat plateau has several small lakes that produce a wetland environment at 12,620 feet and Eldorado Lake came into view with White Dome Mountain at 13,627 feet as a backdrop. Several other mountains showcased their brilliant and dramatic elegance. This was a stunner of a section.

Descending west into Elk Creek, the rock formations changed to quartzite with interwoven thin layers of maroon to blue-gray slate. This descent would take me down nearly 3,000 feet to the Elk Creek hiker stop on the Durango and Silverton Narrow Gauge train. But first, I needed to navigate the steep switchbacks. At the top of this descent, I sat for a long while in the warmer sun that had decided to grace me with its presence. If only my battery life on my camera had lasted long enough, I could have captured just a morsel of this sumptuous vista. The switchbacks looked like a planted garden. I envisioned the Hanging Gardens of Babylon resembling this splendid site.

As I continued my descent, I advanced gradually around the outcrop rock formations that were on the trail. Water was running across the path which made the slate slippery at times. I passed a family who were wearing jeans and garbage bags. How would they handle the cold nights on the mountain? Were they really prepared for what was ahead of them? How I wanted to encourage them to turn around and come back with better equipment at another time. In life, one must know when to share and when to be silent. I was silent that time. That night, I would camp below 10k.

August 4, 2015   *10.9 miles*

Energy gone. I started early but ran out of gas. The last few miles in the Weminuche Wilderness continued descending into the basin. The mountains of the Grenadier Range were among the last peaks to be conquered by mountaineering groups in the 1930s because these peaks required technical skills with the use of ropes. Once I crossed the railroad tracks, I had a five-mile climb.

What a climb it was! One power bar and I was running out of water. Two young men passed me, and then I passed them. They were eating something every time I approached. This went on for the first few miles, and then they vanished. I took a bite of the last power bar with my sip of water. How would I have the willpower to make the top? One foot in front of the other, and a lot of self-encouragement. "You can do this, girl, and guess what? A resupply is waiting for you."

I saw several day hikers, so I knew I was getting close. Into the open with a few muddy crossings, I could hear the traffic on US Highway 550. After reading my clue and checking on the drawing, I decided against entering the private campground at Big Molas Lake. Crossing the highway, I started on another ascent. Where was this bathroom? A page of notes and I couldn't see the bathroom from which I was to start counting paces. I asked a French Canadian about the bathroom. He said, "Just ahead is the bathroom." After hiking a bit further, I turned around and headed back to the highway. I was exhausted, and I hadn't showered in 14 days.

After reviewing the guide, I removed my pack and collapsed my poles. I stuck my thumb out to hitch a ride into Silverton. This would be a Salida repeat. The locals drove past and the motorcycle riders waved. And then, someone stopped - Florida tags. A couple traveling in an RV with their windows up asked, "Need a ride?"

"Yes, please," I was quick to say, "I'm sorry for the smell!"

We chatted for a bit longer as we navigated the roads in Silverton looking for the hostel. There were two parallel roads, so our search was over in minutes. Thanking them, I gave them my information because they wanted to check out Grayson Highlands in Virginia. My home away from home.

Stepping into the small, comfortable reception area, I read the board which listed all the options for staying at the hostel, and the phone number to call since the owner lived upstairs. I had no phone. So, I checked out the bunk room. Several hikers were resting, and they informed me that she had stepped out for the afternoon. An older gentleman said, "Make yourself comfortable." And that's what I did.

I unpacked my things and headed for the shower. I washed and then I washed myself again. It wasn't a two-minute Navy shower! My sister, Mary, always enjoyed her showers, and I took one of hers. Twenty minutes later, I felt clean and was on the prowl for food. The last power bar had done me well. I was among people.

With directions to the only grocery store in town, I dressed up in my feather lite black dress and my flip flops. My sandwich bag held my money and cards which I carried in a zipped pocket on the side of my dress. Walking around the store, I noticed how expensive items were and how they were still selling produce which should have been discarded. I paid for a large bag of chips, spinach dip, a can of soda, and a box of cereal bars, then sat on the porch eating chips and dip. I hoped to find the resupply near Little Molas Lake the next day.

Settling down for the evening, I borrowed a phone to call my mom and my son Eric. After reassuring them that I was doing well, I was ready to complete this adventure and head home to my family.

Since Colorado legalized marijuana, you can smell it every-where. It's not something I require to make me happy. If anything, I'm happy on life. Just the other day, my son Eric and I read a devotional, "Not in the cool crowd?" from the book, *E-mail from God*. It was about Peter and Andrew leaving their fishing nets to follow Jesus. And the remarks about this were as follows, "Some people might even have seen them as rejects, but I (Jesus) didn't. I saw a bunch of ordinary men and women of all ages who weren't afraid to admit they didn't have it all together. They wanted more out of life than posing and pretending everything was alright." Eric and I have realized that sharing is how we heal and it may help others on the way. "Be Free" and be the person you can be. Others around you will do and say what they want. Only you can take control of your life and make it special. I was doing just that with the days remaining on this life-changing undertaking. I can "Be Free" emotionally and physically, and be the real person I am.

August 5, 2015   15 miles

My goal was to finish the Colorado Trail by August 10. Showered and in clean clothes, I was ready to find my food. But first, I walked around this mining town that is something out of a history book. Main Street caters to tourists who want to see things of yesteryear. Brightly painted shops, museums, and restaurants make up this Rocky Mountain town. The Brown Bear Café is a major stop for many motorcyclists who travel out West. It's a charming place that was built in 1893 with bricks that were brought in on the tracks that I had crossed the day before. It opened in the fall of 1893 as a meat and produce market. The upstairs was used by locals to conduct meetings, and later it was remodeled as a restaurant and bar. Sitting at the bar, I had an early morning breakfast. Had the shops been open, I might have spent an extra hour or so.

It was only 8 a.m. and I was anxious to hit the trail. I retrieved my backpack from the hostel and headed out of town. I stood for a good while at the end of town and then decided to move further down the road. I wanted to be away from the fork in the road which headed to Durango. As soon as I relocated myself, someone stopped. I got a lift with the local marijuana shop owner. He had moved from Denver to the quaint community of Silverton, opening his shop on Main Street. Only seventy-four miles to go to Durango, Colorado, and this trek would be a fading memory.

On the trail again, I bushwhacked through a small area that I had hiked yesterday, and all at once, I saw green tape on a tree. Could this be my marker for the resupply? The map and directions were off. But there I was, and I walked down the trail a bit to find the "marshy area." "There is a small grove of trees there," the note said. Nothing looked as the note described. So, I went back to the green taped tree. The note said to look right. I happened to look left and there I saw a bit of the lid sticking out of the ground. How I found it is a complete mystery!

I pulled the bucket out of the ground and headed to the open area because the mosquitoes were attacking me. Working quickly, I repackaged my items, and then placed the remaining food in the bucket by the sign. I had left my stove at the hostel, so I hoped I had packed out enough food. Since I had stumbled onto this part of the trail, I wanted to make sure I was heading in the right direction. I asked a woman, "Which way to Durango?"

On my last leg of the trail, I journaled over and over about how excited I was to be heading home soon. I wanted to see my grandchildren, spend time with my sons, and enjoy a bit of the warm summer before winter came. It was midweek, and the trails were used by many people. The weather was dry, sunny, and warm. A perfect day to be outdoors.

This section would climb steadily for about 11 miles and then descend. The area passed inclined beds of gray shale, sandstone, and limestone. First, I stepped aside as several bikers traveled this section of the trail. Most were day riders who were out before the afternoon thunderstorms rolled in. Mountain biking is very popular in this region. Silverton is a great access point for daily usage of the trail. On this day, I saw two families out with smaller children. Hiking is a great family hobby. My boys were all hiking at a very young age. Eric was five years old when he hiked Mount Snowdon in Wales at 3,560 feet.

Before reaching the boulder cliffs, I hiked in the open and then in the woods for a bit. The wildflowers continued to amaze me. The various shades of yellows and purples were in full bloom. I was able to traverse this vast area with few clouds. In the distance of one boulder field, I saw a waterfall pouring over the massive rock formation. And many evergreens found a foothold in the rocky surface.

Continuing the rocky climb over the top of Peak 12766, I had a million dollar view. I was standing on the red brittle rocks and placed my camera on a rock to pose for a selfie with the view that extended for miles. At this elevation of 12,500 feet, I was still coming across a few snow patches. As I started my descent, I passed four guys in their late twenties. They had gone to college together, and they were out hiking for several days. However, two of them were having a difficult time with the altitude. They weren't sure if they could make it. So, plans were being made to exit on the Fire Service Road in about six miles.

After soaking my feet at a small run-off, I drank and filled my water bottles. Feeling rejuvenated, I went on for a few more miles. As I crossed the bridge on the Cascade Creek, daylight was fading, and it was time to find a place for the night. I went through the trees, and there in front of me was a mountain man. "Hello," he said. He welcomed me to share his campsite. As I was chatting, I quickly scouted for the perfect place. The only other flat area was about six feet from his tent. My antenna went up. Did he roll around on his pad or was he a snorer? He said it was a good thing that I had stopped because the terrain for the next few miles is difficult. A 15-mile day - it was time to sleep.

August 6, 2015   16.5 miles

This was a day that wasn't as memorable as others. I hiked in and out of some wooded areas and found water at some small flowing streams. Unable to come up with words to describe this day on the trail, I have included the few words I wrote that day, "Great day, weather awesome. I did the miles, and now I'm at the watering hole with another SoBo (south-bound hiker). It's only 4:15 p.m. A downhill stretch and I want to do a few more miles. The only catch; there is maybe no water for 22 miles. I drank a liter and packed out 3 liters." I do recall the numerous hummingbirds that flew very close to my head and the runner who gave me a mocha gel. Saving the gel for the next day's climb, I hiked past some young ladies who were hiking a section together. Tired!

August 7, 2015   15.9 miles

I was coming to my final days on the Colorado Trail, and now I'm coming to the end of this writing adventure. I was up early because I was thinking about home and what needed doing. Animals were actively watching me on the trail this day - deer, big-eyed birds, and squirrels that were playing and collecting nuts. A lot of memories about the Appalachian Trail floated through my brain because I was ridge walking in the tree line with views here and there. The sun rose as red as the sand in the Rockies.

On this cooler and cloudier afternoon, I drank only 2¼ liters of water. At one point, I sat under a tree with my plastic bag over me as a thunderstorm passed overhead. After this storm, I continued up the trail. At a relatively fast-moving stream, I met a NoBo (north-bounder), who was lobster red. She was soaking down her body at the first water source on the trail heading north from Durango. She looked dehydrated. Another individual who seemed ill-prepared for this hike. She had exposed her arms and chest to the sun.

I stopped just shy of the very exposed Indian Trail Ridge. With the sun returning, I hoped for a wonderful sunset. As I set up my tent among a few trees, I was excited about seeing the sun fade across the open meadow, but that wasn't the case. As I entered the tent, the sky lit up, and I laid so very flat on my pad. "This is the worst I've ever been in and I'm praying," I recorded in my journal. The rain pelted down all night, and I needed to use the bathroom. What to do? The resourceful person I am, I pulled out a plastic bag and re-lieved myself and then poured it outside the tent door. One must do what one must do in the wilderness.

August 8, 2015   16.3 miles

A sleepless night is what followed that massive lightning storm. It flashed and seconds later the thunder rumbled on. And then it repeated. By early morning, the wind had picked up, and the storm had moved away. I ate my breakfast, hop-ing the tent would dry out a bit before I packed it up. It was much cooler and I could smell fall in the air.

Maverick, whom I had met the day before on the trail, said, "It's the end of summer." It was August 8; that's the middle of summer anywhere else.

My last ridge hike on the Colorado Trail brought back to mind several past hikes. Many years ago, I traveled with my three younger sons and my mom through Wales. One day, we were in a place called "Clouds," and we were walking above the clouds. And the other hike was the European backpacking trip with my son Eric and his father. We camped under the stars outside the old castle walls in Assisi, Italy.

Crossing the rugged, exposed Indian Trail Ridge, I was pushing my body to finish strong. However, I must have looked drained because a hiker returning from his outing stopped and chatted a bit. "You look lethargic," he stated. "I'm tired. I've hiked 20 straight days," I said. He offered me some jerky, and I accepted.

It was a cold but dry stretch which made the rocks passable. As I reached the second summit at 12,258 feet, I saw two hunters out scouting the area. They were both wearing short-sleeved shirts. I had my rain jacket and neck warmer on. After I took a quick selfie, I descended on a steep, rocky trail that led to the first reliable water source in 20 miles. This water flows off a red waterfall, Gaines Gulch.

As I crossed the large wooden bridge, the final climb of the trail was before me. There were several wonderful camp-sites near Junction Creek and only 14.4 miles to Durango. I started the final climb. Half-way up, I thought about those gels I had found way back when. How I could use something sweet! Just then I looked down on the side of the trail by a log, and I found a "Werther's Original" in the wrapper. And yes, this hiker picked it up, and I held it in the corner of my mouth for the first mile. Just like the jerky, I savored it.

Passing a few hikers who had settled down for the night, I reached the top of this last four-mile climb. I set up for my final night on the trail. Placing my tent on the edge of the trail, I staked it down and enjoyed the sunset through the trees. On his way back down the mountain, a local biker rested and ate a snack. We spoke about my hikes and how peaceful it is to be in the wilderness with oneself.

August 9, 2015   *10.3 miles*

Up before the sun, I had enjoyed the best sleep, and the day turned out to be sunny. I started hiking in my long-sleeved shirt and changed at the 3.5-mile mark. It was an early Sun-day morning, and the trail was being used by bikers, hikers, and dog walkers. Only 4.5 miles from the finish, I took a break and sat on a perfectly carved rock chair. I didn't think I could get up off the ground any more. My body was done for. My mind was at peace and I was happy. Smiling again, inside and outside.

Biker: "Hi!"

Me: "Sorry, I was in a daze."

Biker: "Finishing the trail?"

Me: "I am!"

Biker: "Congratulations!"

I came in around 10 a.m. and caught a ride with Ashley, who had moved to Durango because it's such a friendly, laid back town. A dog and young people kind of community. At the welcoming center, I used a computer to book a flight home. I washed up a bit, had a celebration meal and ice cream, and bought a few things for my family. I was ready to go home.

God knows my heart, and I know that I give my all to anything I try. If I make a mistake, I own up to it, and I want nothing more than to help those I can. But I'm unable to make others happy. I'm no longer going to be a victim. I want to "Be Free."

acknowledgements

I have a promise in the Bible that I'm holding on to. That promise is as follows, *"He restores my soul; He leads me in the paths of righteousness for His name's sake."* Psalm 23:3 (NKJV). No matter what the world and others do to us, God restores us. I'm thankful for being able to spend time with Him in the wilderness. He is there to protect and guide me.

Without the encouragement of my publisher and his dedicated family to write another book, I would have only hiked the trail. This family-owned company, Imaging Specialists, believes in my work. My editor, Jessica Cook, took the time to work through my book while raising young children. Tammy Thiele, a dear friend whom I've only met through emails, took the time to read and reflect on the words printed in this book. And she believes that I have several more books in me. I thank you all.

To my sons who have had a rough journey. Thank you for allowing me to share your hurts as well.

To my readers of *Healing, My Journey Home*, who have asked for more books. Thank you for gaining something from my book.

Finally, I want victims to find healing and "Be Free" from the past. Thank you for taking the time to read this book and possibly sharing it with someone who can find peace.

about the author

Meachele "Mothership" Montgomery continues to enjoy her love for hiking with Cianna. Planning to hike the Smokies in May 2016, her new adventure is to build a Tiny House and travel the country with her son, Eric. Working at Footsloggers in Blowing Rock, she continues to share her love and knowledge of backpacking with others. Waiting on Spring, she wants to introduce her latest grandchild, Braxton, to the "Enchanted Forest" of pixies with his older sister, Kayleigh.

Contact Meachele *mothership* Montgomery at:
www.atmothership.~~com~~ net
athiker2011@yahoo.com

Made in the USA
Columbia, SC
29 September 2018